They Call Me Ringler

An Educator's Journey

Mike Ringler

Order Placed On 12 Nov. 2021.

£4·95

Michael A. Ringler

miker345@yahoo.com

Recall 13th October 1981.

Mike Ringler CD's available on CD Baby.com, I-Tunes, and Amazon.com:

"There Comes A Moment" (2012)

"Ringler Road – A Tribute to the Beatles" (2011)

"VI" (2011)

"We Have Liftoff" (2009)

"Note-ified" (2009)

"The Spirit Is The Source" (2008)

"The World Inside My Mind" (2007)

"Writes Of Summer" (2006)

Foreward

My nearly twenty-nine years at Hialeah-Miami Lakes Senior High School provided me the opportunity to work with an amazing array of students, teachers, administrators, and support staff, only a few of whom are included in this book. My intent was neither to write a definitive account of HML, nor discuss every past or present member of the Trojan family, but simply to present the reader with a sampling of some of the people and events that laid the foundation upon which my career in education was built.

A heartfelt thank you to the following people:

My wife Rella; my son Seth; my daughter Penina; my brothers Jeff and Allen; my mom and dad (I know that somehow you're reading the book over someone's shoulder right now); my colleagues past and present; and most of all, the 4,500 or so students who walked into my life and made me a better man.

A special "best wishes" in advance to my friends and colleagues Karen Stemer and Cathy Wanza, two exceptional teachers, who at the time of publication of this book were each in their final year of teaching at HML before retiring. A job extremely well done, ladies!

About Hialeah-Miami Lakes Senior High School

Opening its doors in 1971, Hialeah-Miami Lakes Senior High School, currently one of nearly forty high schools within the Miami-Dade County Public Schools system, and home of the Trojans, primarily serves the children of families from Hialeah, Miami Lakes, and Opa Locka, Florida. Originally, the school's student population was comprised of grades 10 through 12, but in the late 1980's and early 1990's it was expanded to include grade 9 as well, adding an additional 800 or so students, as well as a new building, designated at that time for ninth grade use. With a reputation for strong academic programs and superior athletic teams, "HML" was certainly viewed as one of the finest public high schools in the county. Guided by a succession of strong, experienced principals, anchored by a talented and dedicated faculty and staff, and supported by parents and the overall school community, HML was at the top of its game. By the time I arrived at the school in February 1984, its reputation was fully intact, and for many years it remained a top rated institution.

In 1998, the HSCT, the statewide tenth grade assessment in Reading and Math that students needed to pass in order to later graduate, was replaced by the infamous FCAT. Designed during the tenure of Governor Lawton Chiles, the FCAT was never intended to become the monstrous and mishandled political tool it has since become, but rather, was intended to assess a student's ability to demonstrate "critical thinking" skills, surely a worthwhile goal. So we thought! It wasn't long before the state began using the FCAT results as the primary measurement of a student's, and a school's, academic success. The new school "grade" system, implemented during Jeb Bush's two term stint as governor, rewarded or punished schools with a "report card" grade, based almost exclusively upon the results they achieved on the Reading and Math portions of the FCAT. And of course, students' eligibility to graduate was tied to their FCAT results as well. The misguided pressure was on, and from that point until the present day, schools have been able to focus upon very little besides FCAT, FCAT, and more FCAT. A recent adjustment to the state's school grade program incorporates additional, and very reasonable, factors outside of the FCAT. However, the state itself has not yet been able to effectively calculate the results of some of these factors, including a disastrous failure on the part of the state while grading its newly "ramped up" 2012 version of the FCAT Writing assessment, rendering the new system ineffective and grossly unreliable.

Using FCAT results as the sole measurement, HML began its supposed "decline" by the early part of the new millennium, and continued along the same path through the 2010-2011 school year, (the 2011-2012 report card grade will be released by early 2013), with the school receiving a series of C's, D's, and even one F, under the state's report card grade system. In actuality, the school did amass far more than sufficient points to attain a C grade for 2010-2011, but was penalized one full grade down to a D due to the failure of one target group of a few hundred students to demonstrate a required level of "learning gains", thereby effectively punishing the entire school. This same scenario occurred in the cases of many other schools throughout the state, and will likely continue to haunt schools until the state fully understands the widespread negative ramifications of this nonsensical rule. There are two other major factors which I believe contributed overwhelmingly to HML's downward spiral, the first of which was the opening of Barbara Goleman Senior High School in 1995. Goleman was built to serve students from the northern section of Hialeah, as well as students from Miami Lakes and other nearby areas. As a large number of HML students lived within the newly-shifted borders that would now supply students to Goleman, somewhere in the area of four hundred or so academically strong HML students suddenly found themselves leaving our school and heading a few miles to the north, thus more fully exposing the small "base" of less successful students who had always been at HML, but had been counterbalanced by the stronger group. The second, more disturbing factor which unfairly led to HML's shift was the inclusion of HML in the newly announced "School Improvement Zone" in January 2005. The brainchild of then Superintendent Rudolph Crew, "The Zone" was intended to address the weakness of students in the area of reading by identifying twenty-nine schools that had performed poorly on the FCAT Reading test, extending the length of their school day and school year, and providing targeted instruction in reading skills. From the moment it was announced that Hialeah-Miami Lakes Senior High School had been included as one of the twenty-nine "Zone" schools, the school experienced a steady stream of parents withdrawing their children from HML, unwilling to have their children, most of whom were successful students, subjected to a longer school day and longer school year because of the poor performance of a few hundred other students. Ultimately, this led to the additional loss of hundreds more higher performing HML students, further exposing the reading based weaknesses which the school had been addressing since 1995. As a measure of the failure and immediate impact of "The Zone" upon HML, the school's C grade from the year before dropped swiftly to an F grade by the end of the first year. To my mind, few programs I've seen introduced during my time in Miami-Dade County Public Schools were as unsuccessful as "The Zone".

When a school loses perhaps one fourth of its high achieving student population, leaving behind a suddenly higher percentage of struggling students, that school will undoubtedly suffer. Well, HML has indeed suffered, more than enough! Thankfully, the current principal of the school, Jose Bueno, with whom I had the pleasure of working for my final two years as Language Arts Department Chair, and subsequently, Writing Department Chair, has demonstrated a broader and clearer understanding of the means by which HML may have the opportunity to raise its state school report card grade, and regain at least a degree of its former reputation as a fine school. Were it not for the grade penalty placed upon HML for the 2010-2011 school year, Bueno's first year with us, the school would have received a C, barely missing a B by thirty points or so. The 2011-2012 results, to be released next year, may well bear out that the school has moved even a step higher, but that is yet to be seen. Hope has returned to HML, and the efforts of the faculty, administration, and support staff, are sure to be rewarded in the near future.

Carry on Teacher.
Caning You, Wouldn't tell me, Why You think it is more important to lark about, than attend to your lessons, Would it? Go home and Write me a letter about it.

Prologue

Yes, I loved my students, even the ones who may have deserved it the least. There are many of them from long ago who still remain in contact with me, as do those who were with me during the past few years up until my retirement in June 2012. They email, Facebook message, and call me on the telephone. During my nearly twenty-nine year teaching career at Hialeah-Miami Lakes Senior High School, part of the Miami-Dade County Public Schools system, I had the pleasure (perhaps an exaggeration in a few cases) of teaching approximately 4,500 students, ranging from thirteen to eighteen years of age. I taught , at one time or another, all four high school grade levels, most ability levels, native and non-native English speakers, and children of myriad races, religions, cultures, and socio-economic backgrounds. Considering my lack of previous experience with such a diverse grouping, the one constant that struck me early on was how quickly they all looked the same to me: they were all just kids depending upon me to do something, ANYTHING, to help them get through the days, weeks, and months to come.

I never expected my students to work their way into my heart the way that they ultimately did, but into my heart they silently crept while I worked with them on a daily basis. I learned to recognize their insecurities and their fears, many of which they attempted to conceal behind a veil of *"That's stupid"* or *"Why do we have to learn this* _____ *?"* (you fill in the blank). I tried as hard as I could to see through their facades; to find the strengths, gifts, and talents that each of them surely possessed. Initially, many of them fought me on a regular basis, steadfastly refusing to yield to my attempts to light their fires, and to show them a better way to prepare for the real world that lay just outside the solid brick walls of "HML". Some of them, however, willingly crossed the bridge to "Mr. Ringler's World", no small feat when one is fourteen or fifteen and chooses to defy one's peers. It never took more than just a student or two coming over to my side to convince me that I had indeed chosen wisely when I had decided in early 1984 to leave the world of private industry in order to pursue my original career choice of becoming an English teacher, a career that had been previously put on hold as a result of an apparent nationwide glut of teachers in 1975, the very year I graduated from college.

Refusing at that time to surrender to the hostile environment in which teachers on a nationwide basis were losing their jobs, and proposed openings for teachers were continually being eliminated, I enrolled in a Master of Science degree program, with a concentration in Reading Specialization, at Long Island University's C.W. Post Center, counting on that to enable me one day to secure a teaching position. After being awarded my graduate degree, however, I found myself still on the outside, still in a world that held very little interest for me, other than as a means by which I could take care of my family; a most rewarding undertaking, and one I embraced with all my heart, but one that left me empty career-wise, wondering if a niche in the business world had now become my destiny.

A move to Florida in 1980, followed by yet even more business oriented jobs, further convinced me that my dream of becoming a teacher had all but vanished in the hot, humid, steaminess of the Sunshine State. That is, until February, 1984. Early that month I had read a newspaper article stating that the "worm had turned"; that the decade-long cycle of teacher layoffs had ultimately resulted in the birth of a teacher shortage in many regions of the United States, including South Florida. Without hesitation, I queried both Broward County Public Schools and Dade County Public Schools (not Miami–Dade County back then) as to possible teacher openings, salaries, benefits, etc., and decided that although I lived in Broward County but was already employed by a corporation located in Dade County, and as Dade County Public Schools was offering $3,000 more than Broward for a beginning teacher position, Dade County would be where I would take the step I had initially planned to take in 1975; becoming an English teacher. I quickly submitted all necessary applications and forms, applied for my Florida Temporary Teaching Certificate (Florida had reciprocity with New York State, thus my English 7-12 and Reading K-12 certifications from New York State enabled me to quickly obtain my Florida certification), and in mid-February I went on my one and only interview; meeting with Mr. Don Wilson, principal of Hialeah-Miami Lakes Senior High School. (I had told my secretary the day before that I would be coming into the office a bit late the next morning, taking her by surprise, as I was never, and I mean, NEVER, late to work. I suppose that she might have suspected something, but if she had, she kept it very much to herself, which I of course appreciated as I did not want my staff to become unsettled by any possible uncertainty concerning my continuing with the company.) During our brief interview, Mr. Wilson bluntly asked me what I thought I could bring into the classroom that would ignite a group of basic skills level, 10th grade English II students, and all I could say was that my business experience in private industry would enable me to bring a different part of the "real world" to them; a part that perhaps many other teachers could not relate to from that perspective, and thus could not share with their students. I also pointedly expressed that I would never give up on those students, and that I would hold them to the highest standards with no exceptions; lovingly and supportively, but with no exceptions! Well, apparently, that was all Mr. Wilson needed to hear, as he offered me the job on the spot. Two weeks later, on February 27, 1984, just three days after my thirty-first birthday, I entered Hialeah-Miami Lakes Senior High School for the first time as an – ENGLISH TEACHER!

Through the nearly twenty-nine years that followed, I found myself with an ever-expanding family; a family of young people who trusted me enough to share their lives with me: their joys and their sorrows, their hopes and their times of despair, their successes and their failures. They honored me every day by securing a place in their hearts for me; maybe not all of them, but many. There were those who quickly bought into what I was selling, those who I didn't get until Winter Break or Spring Break, and those who I never got. There were those who took pride in their work, and those who could not have cared less. It amazes me to this day that so many of my students claim that perhaps the most important thing they ever learned from me was the power of their names. Countless times I asked them how in the world they could feel comfortable submitting a sub-standard piece of work on which their name appeared. "You need to understand the power of your own name" was my constant reminder to them of the need to produce their best work. "My God, how can you hand in work that isn't your best when your name is on it? Is that how you want people to think of you when they see your name?" Sometimes my words hit them in just the right place, and sometimes my words passed them by, like a warm, well-intentioned breeze whispering above their heads. Every day, as I stood at my classroom door during the changing of classes, my world was filled with an endless parade of hugs, and kisses, and high-fives, and fist bumps, and "Love you, Mr. Ringler"s, joyfully and lovingly shared with me by my current students, students from previous years, and even by those students who were never actually in any of my classes, but whose friends were, thereby entitling them in their minds to become part of the family.

As each school year came and went, and the unbearably sad ritual of saying goodbye to my students had passed, they and I knew that we would see each other again when the summer had passed, and though they would no longer be in my class, they would always be a part of my family. Those who graduated left knowing that I would always be there for them when they dropped by to visit their old school. I was Mr. Ringler after all, a permanent fixture at HML.

My decision later in the 2011-2012 school year to retire effective that June was a heart-wrenching one to make. How could I leave my kids? Who would be there for them when they need to talk? Who would be standing by my classroom door when they pass by once school is back in session at summer's end? Who would be there to give them a much-needed hug, or words of encouragement when things were just not going their way? How could I do that to them? The answer is simply that as a result of my duties (in a "low-performing" school, as designated by the outrageous school grading system utilized by the state of Florida) as department chairperson of initially the Language Arts Department, and subsequently the Writing Department; combined with teaching my regular full schedule of English and Writing classes; plus dealing with a number of health issues that had been draining my energy level for years; complemented by still having to wake up at 4:30 every morning while approaching sixty years of age; I felt that if I returned for the next school year, I could no longer give my kids and my school 100% of "Mr. Ringler". I knew that if I could not be exactly who I had always been, and could not continue to work at the level of intensity with which I had always approached my position and my profession, it would be better for me to leave than to become a "hanger on"; like an athlete who remains in the game a few years too long, causing long-time fans to say, "He/she was a great_____, but he/she should have left a couple of years ago". I just knew I could never sleep at night thinking that comments like that were floating around, about *me*, somewhere in the universe. So, I informed my administrative staff that I would be retiring in June, filed all of my required paperwork downtown, and told my department(s), and even more painfully, my students, present and past, of my decision. There were shocked faces, and smiles, and tears of both joy and sadness. I found it completely surreal that I had actually said *those* words – "I've decided to retire", but say them I had!

A steady stream of emails, and Facebook messages, and telephone calls, has followed during the first few months of my retirement; from both students and colleagues. I am now on the outside of the world that I tried so hard to build during my career, but those contacts have enabled me to remain connected to it in some fashion. In my other role as a "below the radar" recording artist, I will hopefully return next year to my school in order to perform, as I have done so many times in the past, at the wonderful "Coffee House" fund-raisers organized by the Chorus Department. I'll see my students again, and there will be tears of joy when I arrive, and tears of sadness when I leave, and they will know that they are forever in my heart, and hopefully, just hopefully, I'll always be in theirs.

Chapter 1

"You can't become a teacher; you'll never make any money." Thus spoke my father when I approached him as a college freshman to announce that I did not want to become a dentist. I had originally selected the Pre-Dental major at York College – The City University of New York, at his insistence, though it never felt quite right to me. My first college semester was nearing an end, and truthfully, it had not been a major success for me. I was never a particularly strong student, perhaps less than dedicated would be a more appropriate description, although I was certainly bright enough to be far more successful than my grades indicated. An 80% average seemed to follow me throughout my high school career, with my one attempt at the SAT during my senior year yielding a 1080 score (mid-600's in Reading, mid-400's in Math), barely adequate, but certainly not overly helpful at college application time. If memory serves, my guidance counselor called my parents one time only, a few months before graduation, expressing his concern at my average grades and average SAT results, despite my being a "bright" kid with tremendous potential. A little late perhaps for him to have touched base, but the fault rested squarely upon my shoulders, not his.

While my high school grades were not exactly exemplary, I consistently maintained a 90% or above in my English classes, along with similar grades in a few other qualitative, reading-based courses such as Social Studies and the natural sciences. Algebra, Intermediate Algebra, Chemistry, Foreign Language, and a number of other killers, were the ones that so detrimentally affected my grade average. I clearly remember sitting in some of those classes, listening intently to my teachers, and watching in terror as a variety of concepts went flying above my head on their way past me. I would reach up and clutch helplessly at the air, hoping to grab hold of a concept or two, but alas, the little devils zoomed by, laughing, until they had left me far behind. Of course, the solution would have been to study, either alone or by getting together with a few stronger, more motivated students, but that just wasn't the place in which my academic head resided. I was sure I would get by, more than get by, just on my smarts!

Don't misunderstand; don't be misled. Under the watchful and caring eye of my mother, guided by the powerful and successful presence of my father, and led by the examples of my two older brothers who were respectively pursuing their college and law school careers, I never came to school without my homework, was rarely absent, was never disrespectful to any teacher (certain death at the hands of my parents was sure to follow), and was overall one of the good kids. Teachers liked me. I was helpful and courteous and a gentleman. I was also frequently the class clown, at least in some classes, but when a teacher said, "That's enough Michael", the curtain fell immediately. The consequences at home of a teacher calling to complain about me were too frightening to even think about, so I never needed to be told twice.

I skipped a day of high school once, I swear, only once! It was on my seventeenth birthday in 1971; the day that my junior driver's license was eligible to be converted to a senior license! So, I painstakingly set a devious plan into place. I left for school as usual, but instead of entering the hallowed halls of Benjamin Cardozo Senior High School that day, I boarded the Q-17 bus, headed for the Department of Motor Vehicles in Jamaica, Queens, and beamed as the clerk single-handedly took me from childhood into young manhood with a couple of rubber stamps, and an invitation to step to the side after the much sought-after prize was firmly in my waiting hands!

Those who doubt the existence of a higher power that watches over us and sees all, would surely change their tune if they had been with me on that day. Upon returning home, thankfully uninhabited as my mother was at work, I took the keys to my father's barely less than a year old 1969 Pontiac Catalina, started her up, and proceeded to drive through the vast wonderland that was Queens, New York. I could not believe how accomplished a driver I already wa...BAAMMMMM !!!! "Are you kidding me", I calmly exclaimed after being hit by a large truck in the middle of Long Island City, just as the rush hour was taking its first breaths of the afternoon. (I may have said something a bit more forceful than "Are you kidding me?", but as there will likely be students of mine reading this book at some point, suffice it to say that my memory of my reaction may be somewhat cloudy.) Horns patiently whispering from all sides, accompanied by countless pleasant exhortations to "please move your car, so we can swiftly and courteously drive past you", filled the air and my whirling head. A quick investigation revealed that the massive steel step at the base of the truck door had surgically shorn (sheared, if one so desires) the passenger side of the roof of my father's barely less than a year old 1969 Pontiac Catalina from the remainder of the car's "Body by Fisher". The truth was my only hope, so after getting all pertinent information from the exceedingly friendly driver who had hit me, I returned home, defeated and weary from my first day of senior license driving. I called my father at work to share with him the wonderful news, waited for my mother's impending return home after her workday, and cursed the moment I had decided to skip school that day.

College application day was the moment I had been waiting for through the first six or seven months of my senior year in high school. In New York City Public Schools, the application used for applying to the State University of New York also contains a separate section used to concurrently apply for The City University of New York. Well, with my grades and SAT scores, I received a rejection notice from "SUNY" even before I had submitted my application. "No problem!" I thought. That would just make my decision easier when I had to choose between my first and second choices once I receive my "CUNY" acceptance letter. As Maxwell Smart of "Get Smart" used to say, "Would you believe... ?". Within a month or two of submitting my multi-purpose application, I received a simple post card stating that York College, my *fourth* choice at "CUNY", proudly welcomed me into the York family. Fourth choice ??? I had to check to see where the school was even located, and found that it was the newest of the four-year universities in the "CUNY" system, had two separate campuses a long bus ride apart, and that I would likely be spending time at each. One post card, and I was a "Yorkie"!

Chapter 2

Though I had inwardly thought about becoming a teacher since I was fifteen, my father strongly urged me to pursue a dental career when I entered college; a career I quickly discovered was not the avenue for me. My first indication of that was revealed to me during my first semester, when I was enrolled in College Physics, a course with which I never connected. There went those flying concepts again, the very ones I had last seen passing over my head while I was in high school. My professor, Gary Gerardi, invited me to talk after class one day. He told me that he thought I was exceptionally bright, but that I needed to switch my major as soon as possible, as he just didn't see me in the world of quantitative science. My College Physics course, he said, would be by far the easiest science course within the Pre-Dental track, and I would be better served by pursuing a major that I was truly interested in following, one that would enable me to more fully utilize my talents and abilities. As I had always loved working with kids as a camp counselor, and had always done exceedingly well in my English classes, leading me to think that studying to become an English teacher would be the correct path, I changed my major, and into the world of literature and writing I stepped, with my father's words of warning whispering softly in my ears.

At that time, the war in Vietnam was still raging, the "draft lottery" system used to select nineteen year olds for military service was still in effect, and I would be turning nineteen that February, 1972. Having just had major knee surgery a week after graduating from high school, I felt pretty safe that I would not be drafted, and if I were, that I would never pass the required physical for military service. Plus, my draft eligibility status as a full-time college student was to be "2-S"; deferred due to being a college student. My mother did not buy that for a moment, and was sure that I would be on my way to Vietnam the day after the draft lottery was to be held. Fortunately for me on draft lottery day, the ping-pong ball on which was printed my date of birth, and which held my very fate upon its shiny, white surface as it tumbled and turned inside the spinning drum , was selected as number 293 out of 365 possible birthdays, and I was excluded from military service. A number of my fellow students, and a few other kids I knew from the neighborhood, were not so lucky. Some came back from Vietnam; some didn't!

My life during my first year at York was a dizzying array of catching buses and traveling between two campuses. During both semesters of my freshman year, when I registered for courses seemingly only after every other student in the world had done so, I had courses at one location at 8:00 a.m., traveled to the other campus for a course two or three hours later, then finished my day with classes in the evening. It wasn't until my sophomore year that I began to see some scheduling daylight.

My junior year was the game-changer. Just prior to leaving for Winter Break, the Director of Admissions, Roger Raber, for whom I worked at my part-time school job, informed me that when we returned to school after our brief vacation, there would be a newly hired typist on board. That day came quickly, and I met the new typist, with whom I was instantly smitten. Within a few days, I was introduced to, and immediately fell in love with, her four year old daughter from a previous marriage. My beautiful typist and I were married during Spring Break of my senior year. How clearly I recall completing a major African-American History exam one morning, rushing to gather up my soon-to-be wife and my soon-to-be daughter, and boarding a plane to Detroit where we were to be married. It wasn't that we had selected Detroit because of its universal appeal, it was simply that my wife had grown up there, and much of her family still remained in the Motor City.

Upon returning from my honeymoon, I had but a short few months remaining in college. Graduation was soon a memory, and the daunting task of securing a teaching position began in earnest. I only wish that Earnest had been around to assist me, as there were no such jobs available, at least for a college graduate with a 2.7 GPA. That's right! The same flawed attitude I had about how my smarts would get me through high school, had traveled with me through the first couple of years in college, and once again, I was incorrect. Thus, my low"ish" to average grades from my freshman and sophomore years at York came back to haunt me, preventing the improved grades I had earned during my junior and senior years from lifting my four-year GPA to a more marketable level. As a result, school districts, which faced with decreasing numbers of available positions had had no choice but to require a higher GPA as a minimum requirement for teacher candidates, found me less than a suitable candidate for a teaching position. I was again on the outside, with little to no chance of reaching my goal.

After having sworn to friends and family during my college graduation ceremony that I was finished with school, and would never go back again, I knew I needed to do exactly that in order to improve my chances of becoming a teacher. An advice-seeking telephone call to the New York State Department of Education, resulted in my applying for, and being accepted into, a graduate degree program in Reading Specialization at Long Island University's C.W. Post Center, commencing with the

January 1976 semester. Surely, I had been advised, this would vastly improve my marketability within the world of education. While working full-time for the Helena Rubinstein division of Colgate-Palmolive Corporation, I spent the next two years: evenings, weekends, and summer classes, pursuing my graduate degree, which was awarded to me in February 1978 at a graduation ceremony I was unable to attend due to my responsibilities at work. Teaching position, here I come!

A brief, six-year business career later, after having relocated from New York City to the Great White North of upstate New York for one corporate position, followed by moves to both the west and east coasts of Florida for a variety of additional corporate positions, and the publication of the aforementioned newspaper article about the improving market for teachers in South Florida, I was hired as an English teacher at the also aforementioned Hialeah-Miami Lakes Senior High School, a highly respected school in the Dade County Public Schools system.(I've already described my interview in the prologue, so I won't subject you to that again.) My nine and a half year business career was at an end, and I was about to embark on a journey that would last for nearly twenty-nine years; years during which I worked with eight principals, dozens of assistant principals, hundreds of teachers (a handful of whom became cherished friends of mine), and most importantly, somewhere in the neighborhood of 4,500 students.

Chapter 3

Since 1982, I've lived in Coral Springs, Florida, a beautiful city of approximately 120,000 people. It was incorporated as a city back in the early 1960's, carved out of an incredibly lush section of the Everglades, and until sometime in the 1990's I suppose, was known as "The City in the Country". Unfortunately, it is less than conveniently located thirty-five miles north of Hialeah-Miami Lakes Senior High School, which resulted in my spending a great deal of time and money traveling back and forth to work. Work! It's funny, but I never said I was going to work, only that I was going to school! Teaching was the hardest job I'd ever had, but I just didn't see it that way. There were times I couldn't believe I was being paid to read and discuss literature with kids; trying to get them to willingly enter a world that would take them to places far beyond South Florida just by turning a few pages. It usually took a while for my students to allow my literary ramblings into the deepest recesses of their minds, but when they did, it was amazing!

Having been born and "white" bred in Bayside, Queens (one of the boroughs of New York City), and attending public school from elementary through high school in that predominantly white neighborhood, my experience with the Latin community was indeed limited. My years at York College, the main campus of which was located in the overwhelmingly African-American town of Jamaica, Queens, had successfully exposed me to the richness and beauty of the African-American culture. And while my previous work experience had brought me in contact with a wide variety of people from a wide variety of backgrounds, none of these factors had prepared me for the world I entered on February 27, 1984. As I hurriedly passed through the doors of the main entrance to HML, it was all too clear that I had never been *here* before. There were plenty of kids speaking English of course, but there were also many speaking Spanish, with a few conversing in Haitian-Creole, a lesser few speaking in what, I later discovered, was Urdu, and a lesser, lesser few speaking any number of other languages . I immediately wondered what the students in my classes would be like, though I had been previously advised that they were a widely diverse group. Wending my way through the flowing student hallway traffic, I climbed the stairs leading to the "English" area on the second floor, found the pair of side-by-side classrooms in which I would be teaching for the remainder of that year, confidently entered Room 215, and for the very first time, wrote my name, "Mr. Ringler", on the blackboard.

"Are you our new teacher?" "Are you taking over for Mr. Jaworski?" "Are you mean?" These were the first questions I had to answer, the first of surely tens of thousands of questions I would answer during my career as a teacher. "Yes, I'm your new teacher."; "Yes, I'm here to replace Mr. Jaworski."; and "Yes, I'm very mean!". I had always felt that I could have been a fairly successful actor, based primarily upon my two brief stints in my elementary school drama club and nothing more. Whatever acting prowess I possessed was quickly called to the forefront, to become a most significant tool as I searched for ways to connect with my students; on that day, and for the remainder of my time at HML. As I watched their faces react to each of my answers, especially the one about my being mean, I saw exactly how much like little children they looked to me. Yes, they were tenth graders, aged fourteen or fifteen, and thought of themselves as adults, but their "I'm still a little kid on the inside" looks, for better or for worse, were clearly showing through on their faces; most vividly in their eyes. They were white, black, Asian, and Middle Eastern, some from Florida, and some from other countries, newly entered into the United States, but now all in my hands, and very soon, in my heart.

Prior to my first day as a teacher, I had decided that if I wanted to maintain a well-managed classroom, I would need to bring my New York attitude into class with me. I was a tough guy! I had responded quickly and effectively to the occasional physical threats directed at me in junior high and high school. Kids back then knew not to mess with Mike Ringler. Each year before school started, my mother told me that if she ever received a telephone call from school stating that I had started trouble, life as I knew it would end. Yet, she also said that if someone desired to physically start with me, and I couldn't peacefully talk my way out of it, I was to make them sorry that they had been born. That is, only if they had struck first. "You're nobody's doormat", she reminded me every year. So, when the need arose, I took care of things my way. Don't get me wrong, everyone knew that I was the friendliest, funniest kid around, and that I would help anybody who had a problem. I just refused to give in to threats. Well, that was going to be my approach as a teacher. My classroom would be *my* classroom, and I would welcome my students into it as long as they could adhere to my rules of decency and respect. None of this actually translated into my being mean, just firm, steadfast, and consistent. I demanded that they refrain from using profanity. Yes, I knew all of the words; I used many of them myself outside of school, when appropriate. I just wasn't about to hear them in class.

Before the first week had ended, I had broken up my first fight in class, the first in a long line of fights I would break up over the years. A tall, stringbean thin boy named John had slapped a girl in the face, an action which she did not take kindly. As I stepped in between them, John aggressively placed his hands on my chest, attempting to move me out of the way. A moment later, while John was closely examining the material I had written upon the blackboard, the security monitor assigned to the second floor who had been summoned via the little red button located at the front of every classroom, arrived to escort young John to the office of the appropriate assistant principal for disciplinary action. My students were still buzzing about the brief skirmish when I turned to them and said it was time to get back to what we were doing. They could see that I was not going to allow anyone, or anything, to prevent us from moving forward. In the eyes of my students, and the other students with whom they would surely speak about this incident, I was clearly not the teacher in front of whom one should start a fight. That newly-established reputation helped me on numerous occasions thereafter, enabling me to de-escalate brewing altercations before they fully erupted. My involvement in occasional, future similar situations during my time at HML acted to re-establish and further solidify that reputation, which to me, was the most effective means by which to prevent more frequent such occurrences from erupting. The older I became, the more grateful I was for this.

Thankfully, it was business as usual for the remainder of my first year, during which I had become close to a number of my students. On many occasions, my students would raise questions about "stuff" that had little or nothing to do with the actual material being covered, but which was obviously important to them. Well, if it was important to them, it was important to me. Why had I become a teacher in the first place? Was it simply to deliver material to them, or was it to help them grow, and become more confident and intellectually curious?

Deciding upon the latter, I would stop my regular lesson and the area in question would become the point of discussion. Every student was invited to participate, and I made sure to call upon even those who wished to remain silent. They could refrain from speaking about the topic, but they at least had to tell me that they "didn't know". I had to hear their voices. *This* was the way, *this* was the method by which I could gain their trust. I saw it so clearly. If they knew, really knew, how much I respected their ideas and their input, and their willingness to speak up, they would see that I was someone to whom they could go when they needed to talk. Their problems were my problems, they mattered to me as people, they were part of my world and they mattered.

Having started my first year in February, things just felt incomplete when the year ended. Sadly, Don Wilson, the principal who had hired me, passed away during that first summer. Bill Noble, a jolly, good-natured fellow whom everybody would soon grow to love, was brought in as principal, the position he held for the next six years. My second year, in which I taught multiple grades, brought me the first group of students who would be mine from start to finish. A number of them, including Miriam, Jackie, Arturo, Larry, Oscar, and Sean, connected with me quickly, thus helping me to reach my other students more effectively. They led, and the others followed. Miriam, a painfully shy, but wonderfully sweet, ESOL student, attached herself to me, eventually telling me all about her life, her family, her relocation from Cuba to the United States, and her goals for the future. She was such a good student, and I hated to see her go at the end of the year. Happily, Miriam was to be my student during her remaining two years in high school. I will never forget the look of sadness on her face when the school yearbooks had arrived towards the end of her senior year, and many of her classmates were looking through their copies in class. Her family just didn't have the money to buy her one, and it broke my heart to see her like that. One day, I asked her to call her parents to ask them if they would be offended if I bought her a yearbook. "They would not be offended at all", she said after she had hung up the telephone in the English Office. I asked how she felt about my wanting to do this for her, and the tears in her eyes were all the answer I needed. After class, I walked over to the Journalism room in which the yearbooks were sold, paid the $30.00 or $35.00 (I honestly can't remember the exact amount), and was given a fresh, inky-smelling copy to bring to Miriam. As the final bell sounded the end of another school day, I met Miriam at her locker and presented her with the yearbook. She cried, and hugged me for a few minutes, leaving my button-down oxford dress shirt wet, and streaky with a bit of black eye makeup. I felt as if we were both acting in a movie, but it wasn't a movie, it was real, and I had made a difference in a kid's life.

Dear Teacher,

The time came to end all those good times in your Reading and English class, but I won't say goodbye but see you soon and I won't ever forget you or your kindness and your caring about me and my problems. You were not just my teacher but you were my friend. That's a friendship I will always treasure. I will come visit you soon and try not to forget me. I won't ever forget you.

I wish all the best for you and your loved ones.

P.S.   I never forget the day when you bought me the yearbook. One day I will visit you and paid for that.

All my love,

Mirita

While with me as tenth graders during that second year, Larry and Sean, both members of HML's extremely successful basketball team, asked me if I would like to stick around after school to play ball with them, and a few other members of the team. Having been a reasonably good basketball player myself during my high school years, and having been asked by York College's head coach back in January 1971 to try out for the York College team that June as he was sure he could use me, I agreed to play ball with my kids. (As luck would have it, bad luck that is, two weeks after being asked by York's coach to try out for the team, the anterior cruciate ligament (ACL) in my left knee was completely torn in two during a basketball game, compounded by multiple cartilage tears, and my chance to possibly play ball for York was gone. Surgery that July, and a year or so of recovery and therapy did enable me to play ball again, but never at quite the same level, and certainly not as often due to ever-increasing swelling, and the onset of arthritis in the knee.) It was quite an honor for me to have been asked to hang with these kids. I was a thirty-two year old white guy, and their teacher to boot, but these great kids, both of whom were black, actually wanted me to spend time with them after school. Somehow I was connecting with them in a way that transcended standard teacher-student protocol, and that was both new, and incredibly heartwarming to me.

Chapter 4

Hialeah-Miami Lakes Senior High School was pretty legendary by the time I arrived in 1984. It had always been near the top of the Dade County Public Schools list, both in the areas of athletics and academics. 1986 brought a state championship in basketball, preceded in 1985 by a national championship in baseball, thanks to a final inning home run by Arturo, one of my students. More than anything, however, HML was known for its outstanding faculty. As a member of the English Department, long before the nationwide transition of English departments becoming relabeled as Language Arts departments, I had the pleasure of working with a number of incredible teachers. These were teachers whose names were known in other high schools around the county, teachers on the short list of "wanna haves" of every hardworking and successful student in the school: Ray Harrell, Gary Graziani, Sue Kropf, Patty Borcz, Lucy Felice, Anne Salvo, Karen Stemer, and Cathy Wanza, among others. They were "old school" English teachers. They brought great literature to life, and held their students fully accountable for every word of it. There was no FCAT to fret about, no time wasted preparing for such misguided and erroneous measurements of accountability, which were later to be foisted upon a well-intentioned, but sadly misinformed public in Florida. There was literature, and writing, and class discussion; all of the components necessary to open the minds of students. Their students were alive with intellectual curiosity, and were encouraged by these great teachers to explore, and question, and reach higher. Some may argue that the students were simply stronger back then, and to some degree, that may be true. But mandates and an endless array of visionary programs at the district, state, and federal levels, introduced and then ultimately discarded for the next great idea, corralled the need for thinking, replacing it with the need to demonstrate proficiency on standardized tests as measurements of student success.

There were other teachers with whom I worked, some during my first few years, some later on, and some in my final years at *HML*, who were notable for any number of reasons. A few of them were simply outstanding educators, and their students knew how fortunate they were to have had them as teachers. Teachers like Michael Garcia, Jorge Deleon, Ann Zirkle, and Barbara Garcia.

Michael Garcia joined our faculty a few years after I arrived, another in a long line of new English teachers. A graduate of HML, Michael was living the dream of many young teachers; having the opportunity to teach at the same high school from which they had graduated. It became quite clear within a few years that he was destined to become one of the finest English teachers in the school, eventually to take his place in the pantheon of HML's best. His forte was, and remains, all things Shakespeare. As the "old guard" of teachers retired one by one, Michael moved more and more into the areas of Honors and Advanced Placement English courses, and has recently become an integral component of the new and expanding "Dual Enrollment" program, wherein students are able to take college courses concurrently with their high school courses. With a few more years to go before he too rides off into the sunset, those students who are lucky enough to see the name Michael Garcia on their new class schedule, will be, as so many before them, entranced by this dynamic teacher.

Surely one of the most dedicated and powerfully inspirational teachers I've ever known was Jorge Deleon, a member, and eventual department chair, of the Foreign Language Department. Though Jorge left our school a number of years ago for another high school located much closer to his home, one where he would be able to oversee his own children's educational progress, he was truly a well-loved and well-respected member of our faculty. He had a fiery passion for his Spanish speaking students, many of whom were, or would be, mine as well during my time as ESOL Department Chair. He watched out for them like a hawk watching over its young, demanding their best effort at all times, while fiercely defending them against the elements of prejudice that pervaded the minds and hearts of some students, and in rare instances, a faculty member or two. In many ways, he reminded me of...*me*! He was a Spanish speaking version of me. We had such similar ideas about teaching foreign speakers, about holding them to the highest standards while being there to protect and console them as they tread the rough road to language fluency. Towards the end of the 1998-1999 school year, a number of the students we both shared came to ask me if they could use my classroom for an after-school award presentation they had planned for Mr. Deleon. Of course, I was glad to let them use it, and offered to help in any way I could to get him to my room. On that particular day, a couple of students came to my office as soon as school had ended, asking me to join them in my classroom for the presentation. Upon my arrival, I found Jorge already there, along with about forty of our kids. One representative of the group stood at the front of the room and thanked Mr. Deleon for everything he had done for his students that year. The real surprise came next, as he then also asked me to stand up and come to the front of the room. Unbeknownst to me, the presentation was planned for both Mr. Deleon and Mr. Ringler! Those wonderful kids wanted to thank me as well for all of the support, guidance, and dedication I had given them that year. I was extremely touched by that, and quite proud to receive one of the twin beautiful plaques that the kids had paid for on their own. Jorge and I stood together, with our arms resting upon each other's shoulders, knowing that we were of the same mind and the same spirit, and how lucky we were to have such hard working and appreciative students. Jorge was a great man, and I missed working with him after he left.

In the last stage of my career at HML, a young teacher joined the Social Studies Department. Her name was Barbara Garcia, though everyone quickly came to call her Barbie, just like the namesake doll she was. She was tiny in stature, but had the heart of a warrior. Students who might have thought she was going to be an easy one to outmaneuver were immediately stopped dead in their tracks. Barbie's reputation grew, almost overnight, as a teacher who would hold students to the fire, demanding their best work, or have them face her wrath. She was, and still is, a kind-hearted and generous woman, but when she was in teacher "mode", all bets were off. A couple of years before my retirement, Barbie was appointed Social Studies Department Chair, as that position had become available. On more than one occasion, she came to see me, or sent me email messages, seeking advice and guidance on the best way to handle her new leadership duties. Happily providing her with every suggestion I could muster, I found her to be a most willing student. She wanted to be the most successful leader she could, and I was so honored to be asked to take her step by step through the process. Watching her develop into one of our finest department chairs was certainly one of the most rewarding experiences I'd had at HML. During my final week at school, Barbie sent me a beautiful, heartfelt email message, thanking me for having helped her become a better department chair, and for always supporting and reassuring her during her moments of doubt. When I saw her later that day, I hugged her and told her how proud I was of her. Then I turned to go, confident that my school was in good hands for another generation.

Another teacher who followed the path of returning to HML years after graduating was Ann Colucci, one of the school's most beloved mathematics teachers. Upon joining our faculty, I believe it was in 1998 or 1999, Ann quickly established herself as a quiet but rigorous instructor, eventually becoming one of the mainstays of the Math Department. Teaching primarily advanced level math courses, the very ones in which I would never have had a chance to succeed during my high school days, Ann somehow presented the most complex material in a way that was "graspable" by her students. Ten years or so ago, Ann (now Zirkle thanks to her marriage to husband Justin) was told that she had breast cancer. Though I do not have all of the details about her case, it seemed that the disease was fairly advanced, and would be treated aggressively. Chemotherapy, followed by a double mastectomy, followed by radiation and medications, gave us all hope that Ann had indeed beaten back this deadly attacker, but ultimately we were wrong. With a level of courage and dignity that I had never personally witnessed before, Ann fought this disease with the heart of a lion, though nary a roar was heard. She complained to no one, choosing instead by sheer will to fight quietly, without calling undue attention to herself. She and Justin eventually adopted a beautiful little boy, Christopher, and proceeded to raise him as any wonderful, loving parents would do. Justin and Christopher surely became her reason to fight, and fight she did. Though on more than one occasion, this evil specter tried its best to take her, she would simply not be taken, not yet. I clearly recall a moment a few years ago, when Ann and I were proctoring the FCAT in adjoining rooms and the testing materials had just been collected, but the students were required to remain in their testing rooms for a while longer. As she and I stepped outside our testing rooms, seeking a temporary respite from the FCAT scenario, I told her that she was my hero. I explained that I had very few such heroes, my father being my primary example, and that I never expected to have such a young woman as my hero, but that was the way I felt. I was in my fifties, and she was in her thirties, young enough to be my daughter, but inspirational enough to be my hero. She blushed, thanked me for my kind words, and stepped over to gently hug me before returning to her soon-to-explode-from-the-boredom students. On August 16, 2011, just a week prior to the beginning of the new school year, Ann passed away, leaving an unfillable hole in the very heart of HML. We were devastated, and shocked that our little Ann Colucci had left us, and her beautiful family. To deal with the loss, I wrote and recorded a song, "Memories Of An Angel", an mp3 copy of which I forwarded by email to Ann's husband Justin. Within an hour he replied, saying how touching and comforting the song was, and how he had forwarded it to Ann's sister, another HML graduate, as well as Ann's mother. The next day I received her sister's reply, in which she promised that Ann's son Christopher, along with her own children, would hear the song as a reminder of the amazing person Ann was. Just in time for Christmas, with the assistance of David Ruiz, teacher and sponsor of our school's TV news program, a video comprised of an array of photographs featuring Ann, Justin, Christopher, and the rest of her family, and using my song as the music track, was produced and presented to the entire school via our in-house TV system. I then made two DVD copies of the video and mailed them to Justin, for which he, and the rest of the family, were exceedingly grateful. Our Ann lives on in those images, and in that song, and in the hearts and minds of every member of the HML family.

And then there's Graz, a teacher who resided within the walls of his own fortress, and who simply must be discussed at this moment. One of the aforementioned old-timers, Gary Graziani, or "Graz" as he was known throughout the school, was a world unto his own. Ten years and ten days older than I was, he was the son of a famous Miami area restauranteur, had long ago left the family business far behind, and had been both delighting and confounding English students ever since. Stubborn, illogical, less than organized, and emotionally trapped in a past which he never seemed comfortable leaving behind, Graz became one of my two closest friends at HML. It was an odd pairing: a man who was en route a thousand years ago to a career as a Catholic priest until he met his future wife, and a Jewish guy from New York City. To compound the situation, he was a staunch Republican and I was a staunch-er Democrat. My God, the political arguments we had during lunch! Actually, our entire "lunch bunch" would frequently become involved in these "differences of opinion". Over the years, as some of the walls surrounding Graz began to crumble, he stepped lightly towards the center politically, as his big heart gradually got the better of his big mouth. As an English teacher, he was truly loved by his students. His passion for literature seemed to emanate from his very soul, and his students clearly recognized that. He would often pace around his classroom, somewhat like a mad scientist, quoting and excerpting, and yes, rambling, about the literary piece being studied at that moment. Students were mesmerized, confused, perhaps a bit frightened, but they would more likely than not come to understand where he was going. We all felt that way about Graz. His discussions traveled in multiple directions, sometimes with an end point, sometimes with no end point in sight, and sometimes with a possible endpoint far off to the distant left or right, hidden behind a trail of convoluted logic that required the listener to exhibit unearthly levels of patience and puzzle-solving skills to follow.

Every member of HML's faculty and staff eventually came to know that Graz depended upon me for the "nuts and bolts" of our job: using the computer, registering for professional development courses, completing insurance enrollment forms and teacher recertification forms in a timely fashion, keeping track of various passwords, and numerous other "real-world" tasks. My God, I even kept a "Graz" file containing all of his information, tucked securely inside my attache' case and carried with me until long after he had retired. On more than one occasion, Graz would come to my classroom and ask me what his password was for this or that. When the time arrived for Graz's departure from HML, his biggest concern was how in the heck he was going to take care of all of the "stuff" he had depended upon me to handle, or remind him of, and he made it quite clear that he would be calling me about such things as the need arose. Like Cher, and Michael, and Bruce, the single name Graz became legendary. No additional identifier was necessary; just Graz!

Chapter 5

Anyone who knows me, knows that I am a rock and roll fanatic. To me, The Beatles sit alone upon the highest throne, with a limited number of bands and artists occupying the tier just below them, followed by dozens of others that complete the rock pantheon. As a drummer since age fifteen, I had often times longed to play in a band, but had never really pursued that path, that is until 1986, when I first met Carlos Llopis, a Hialeah police officer who was assigned to HML as the school's "resource officer". Though I can't precisely remember our first meeting, I'm sure it was simply a passing "hello" as I made my way through the halls of the school. During our earliest conversations, however, we soon discovered that we had something in common; an intense love for The Beatles. Carlos revealed to me that he was a guitarist, and had played in a variety of "Beatles-themed" bands over the years, almost all of which included his good friend Gino. In the mid-1980's, HML began hosting an annual "Star Night" event, featuring a variety of acts comprised of students, faculty, and anyone else who cared to participate. One day in early 1986, Carlos suggested that I meet another friend of his, Steve Kwarciak, HML's then current band director and a guitarist. With my friend and English teacher colleague Mike Murray joining in, the four of us sat down one day after school, discussed the possibility of our "jamming" in the Band Room, and my long held desire to be in a band was about to be fulfilled. Our first goal: "Star Night 1986".

I soon found myself in a bit of rock and roll heaven. Carlos sounded almost exactly like John Lennon. Augmenting Carlos's solid rhythm guitar playing was Steve K. on lead guitar, a fine player with a broad based knowledge of many classic rock tunes, and the skill to bring that knowledge to life. Mike Murray handled bass guitar, while I, despite not having played drums for many years, quickly regained my natural skill set, while discovering that I apparently had a pretty effective rock and roll singing voice. In short order, the four of us were playing high quality renditions of some of our favorite Beatles tunes, along with songs by a variety of other bands like The Doors, Led Zeppelin, and Deep Purple, all of which I had the honor of singing. We decided that we should play a few songs at "Star Night", leading me to register the four of us as participants. When asked under what name we would be playing, I said I would have to check with the rest of the band. When I suggested the name "Old Age", mainly as a joke due to three of us being in our early thirties (Steve K. was in his late twenties), the name stuck. "Old Age" we were, and "Old Age" we would remain for the next four years.

When our moment arrived at the 1986 "Star Night", it was obvious that the six hundred students and faculty in attendance expected nothing more than a group of guys playing "air guitars and drums", possibly lip-synching to a pre-recorded soundtrack. When the chords to Deep Purple's "Smoke On The Water" exploded from Steve K.'s glossy black Gretsch, it was clear that this would be something far different than that. We played three tunes that night, and the audience was fairly well stunned. They cheered and stamped their feet, and provided us with a much appreciated standing ovation for quite a few minutes. The very next day, a group of students formed an "Old Age" fan club, and for the remainder of that year and the three years that followed, we proved that rock and roll was indeed at HML to stay. Another member of the faculty, chorus director Karol Graser, had joined us for our second year's performance, as did Carlos' friend and band mate Gino, both of whom remained vital members of the band for the duration. My time as a member of "Old Age" was a beautiful time, a time filled with friendship and great music and the realization of a childhood dream that might have otherwise been lost forever. Years later, when I was asked to fill in for the drummer in Carlos and Gino's "real" band "Justus", just for a one night gig at the Eden Roc hotel in Miami Beach, I jumped in head first and the dream took a major leap forward. Weeks of "catching up" led to a well-received band performance, and I was asked to join the band permanently. Already in my early forties, and not being at all a "night person", I hesitantly accepted the offer after running the idea past my wife, and played with them for a year, sadly departing the band when the time requirements became too much for me to handle while fulfilling my duties as ESOL Department Chair at HML. For that year, however, "Justus" made a mark on the South Florida music scene, playing at a number of desired venues and ultimately headlining at Christmas and New Year's Eve events in the Miami area. I loved playing and singing with my band mates, and thrived on the energy of the audiences, but found my own energy level constantly depleted. My job had to come first, and so, having taken my childhood dream much further than I had intended, I stepped aside. Happily, as I have been writing and recording my own music since 2005, with eight albums to date on I-Tunes and other music services, the dream continues. How many musicians who have started to record albums while in their fifties have their songs played on radio stations in Australia, Canada, England, Japan, and The United States? As a result of being the composer, sole musician, recording engineer, and public relations guy, I answer to nobody but me. I do miss my band mates though, so occasionally I will disagree with myself while recording an album, just to add a little spice to the process.

Speaking of Mike Murray, well, he was one of the most unusual characters I had ever met. Mike was hired as an English teacher at HML the year after I arrived, and also served as an assistant coach of our baseball team, a position he held throughout most of his four years at the school. Originally from the Boston area, Mike had recently moved with his wife to Dade County from the west coast of Florida. He and I shared a love for many of the same bands, and so it was inevitable that we would soon become friends. As Mike and his wife had one car, which she needed for her longer trip to work each day, and as they lived a short distance from HML, I volunteered to pick him up in the morning on my way to school. As he frequently had to remain after school for baseball practice during the season, he would usually have one of his coaching colleagues drop him off at home afterwards, but otherwise, he rode with me. As we became closer friends, Mike and I would spend a great deal of time talking about music, sharing albums with each other, and in later years, even writing a series of silly songs about our teacher colleagues that we eventually assembled into two individual albums under the band name "The Offenders". Mike appeared to live his life at two speeds: reasonably laid back, and explosive. He could be polite and gentle, and under the wrong circumstances, could quickly metamorphose into a raging bull. I saw both sides of Mike on many occasions, and it was clear that his gentler half was the more frequently displayed side, but there were definitely some Mike Murray moments that bear repeating.

When recording the songs we had written about our teacher friends, we would usually begin by recording Mike playing a basic guitar track. I would then take that track home with me, and through the magic of multi-track recording, I would add other instruments and vocals, mixing the songs down to a standard cassette format once completed. Copies of the final tapes were made for distribution throughout the English department, with the original remaining with me and the first copy going to Mike. One early morning as we drove to HML, Mike wanted to play one of our songs from a cassette he had brought from home. Unknown to Mike, his two year old daughter had switched that cassette with one of her own, placing her tape in our cassette case, and our tape in hers. Imagine our surprise when Mike popped the cassette into my car's tape deck, awaiting the melodic tones of The Offenders, but instead, hearing the opening bars of a children's song. I'd never before thought about how many pieces an exploding cassette might yield, but I soon had a very definitive idea. Ejecting the cassette from the tape deck while simultaneously uttering a few very choice words, Mike grabbed it and forcefully threw the tape out of the car window, only to discover one minor flaw in his plan; the window was still up! Being a stocky and powerfully built man, Mike was possessed of great strength. With pieces of formerly intact cassette sailing in front of my face as I drove, and Mike now red-faced and embarrassed, I could not contain myself any longer. I burst out laughing, trying to explain that it really wasn't that big a deal that his daughter had switched the cassettes, she was two years old for God's sake, and to please check to make sure the window was down if he ever wanted to throw something out of it in the future.

I thought for sure that Graz was going to end up a quadriplegic. Mike Murray, all two hundred and thirty some odd pounds of him, had just launched himself into the air towards Graz, like a kid playing leapfrog, landing squarely on Graz's neck. I don't think the human neck is designed to bend at a ninety degree angle in any direction, but I, along with a few of my colleagues, watched in horror as Graz's head snapped down, chin planted firmly on chest, as Mike completed his acrobatic maneuver and now stood in front of the white as a sheet Graz. "Oh my God" was but one of the exclamations heard from the lunch bunch, with many more richly detailed expressions ringing off of the walls of the English Office. Fortunately, Graz was still alive, and could feel his arms and legs. Concerned, Mike asked his shocked victim how he was, profusely apologizing over and over for his less than stellar decision, and we all resumed our mid-morning meal, my visions of a wheelchair bound Graz fading with each passing moment. After that incident, I don't think Graz, or anyone else for that matter, ever turned their backs to Mike; you just never knew when it was coming.

Chapter 6

Prior to the beginning of the 1987-1988 school year, my third full year at HML, my department chair Ray Harrell left to teach at the School For Advanced Studies, a very high level program at Miami-Dade Community College, wherein academically superior students would attend both high school and college at the same time. Ray was a superior English teacher, and this program was a perfect fit. The plan was for him to spend one year there, and then return to HML. This sudden move left my department with the need to elect an interim English Department Chair, no easy task within a department of thirty teachers. Though I had only been a teacher for two and a half years, apparently a number of department members felt that with my prior business and management experience within the corporate world, I would be a good choice to hold down the fort for the year that Ray was to be gone. There were two other candidates as well, either of whom would have done an outstanding job, but when the voting was over, and the smoke had cleared, I was the choice to lead the department.

At age thirty-three, after having left leadership positions far behind me when I left private industry, I was back in that role, if only for a year, as Interim English Department Chair. I was not overwhelmed or hesitant about what I needed to do in Ray's absence. I simply had to maintain, to fulfill the duties of the position by keeping the department moving forward as smoothly as possible to ensure an easy return for Ray the following year. As I was still learning my craft as an English teacher, and had nowhere near the extensive literary background as Ray, and even a number of my department members, I decided to appoint grade level chairpersons for each grade. I charged them with the responsibility of directing the curriculum, and conducting meetings for their grade level colleagues in addition to the full department meetings I would hold each month. As that year's teaching assignments had been determined by Ray prior to the end of the previous school year, at least that was out of the picture. Of course, I would have to handle that task later in my interim year, but that was not something with which to concern myself at the moment. Things went fairly smoothly that year. Our state HSCT Reading assessment results went up, and I somehow managed to bring my department (which had a tendency to be divided philosophically into two distinct camps) a bit closer together, by no means a simple task. The final days of school meant that Ray would soon be returning to the department, and I would be back to being able to concentrate exclusively on my teaching.

People who hold leadership positions are occasionally called upon to make sense of tragic events; to provide some degree of comfort and stability to the members of their staff. One sad event during my year as Interim English Department Chair thrust me squarely into that arena. Wallace Merrell, a very young, soft-spoken, highly effective English teacher who had served at HML for the previous three years, had transferred during the summer to a middle school much closer to his Homestead home, thus reducing his seventy-five mile round trip to HML to a more agreeable total of three miles. "Wally" was married to Elizabeth, and had two (if I remember correctly) very young children at home. He was a loving husband and father, and he wanted to be able to spend more time with his family. Wally's absence from our department was all too glaring, and we all missed his unusual sense of humor and dry wit. One morning, while working in my office, the telephone rang. Nery Fins, another very young and very talented English teacher who happened to be in the office with a few other members of the department, answered the telephone and within seconds, had turned as white as a ghost. "Ringler. It's Elizabeth. Wally died!" I immediately took the telephone from Nery and asked Elizabeth what had happened. Between sobs, she explained that Wally had had a severe allergic reaction after having eaten some nuts that had been given to him by a co-worker. He apparently was driving home after school the afternoon before, ate some of the nuts, and began to have severe difficulty breathing by the time he reached his house. Elizabeth immediately had Wally back in the car, and sped off to the local hospital, no more than a mile or so away. In the few minutes it took to reach the hospital, certainly far faster than it would have been to summon an ambulance and await its arrival, Wally went into anaphylactic shock, and simply stopped breathing. Upon her arrival at the hospital, Elizabeth frantically summoned help at the front desk of the emergency area, but Wally was already gone. He was only in his late twenties, and yet, however unfairly, he was gone. Before our conversation was over, she told me that she needed some guidance regarding Wally's school life insurance and any possible social security benefits. Knowing that neither the school district nor the Social Security Administration office would discuss these things with me, I provided Elizabeth with a variety of district telephone numbers and one for Social Security as well.

The members of my department were deeply saddened by Wally's death, and I spent many hours discussing him with them. They were understandably concerned about Elizabeth and the children. I explained that Elizabeth was a strong young lady, and that while speaking with her that morning, I knew she would somehow pull herself and her children through this unfathomable loss. At times such as those, it's incredible how petty differences and opposing philosophies are so easily set aside. There we were, thirty educators of all ages, from a wide array of backgrounds, and the only thing that mattered was how we could best assist the family of a young man who no longer even worked with us.

With Elizabeth at home as a full-time mother, and with no income to support the family, I knew that she would now be faced with the daunting task of handling all financial obligations. An informal donations fund was quickly established, and people both within and outside of the school contributed what they could to assist Elizabeth and the children. When we had collected all of the donations, I drove to Homestead to deliver the contributions to Elizabeth. We talked for a while, and then I drove the sixty miles back to my home. For the next year or so, Elizabeth called me on occasion to bring me, and the department, up to date on her family's progress. A few years later, she telephoned me at home to let me know that she had met a wonderful man, a sergeant currently stationed at Homestead Air Force Base, and that they would soon be getting married. I was thrilled to hear such wonderful news, and immediately shared it with my department the next morning. After she had remarried, I heard from her one final time. She told me she and the children were doing well, that her husband was a good man, and that they would possibly be moving to another base. She thanked me for stepping in to help during that terrible time, and that she was happy that Wally had had the chance to work with such a wonderful and caring group of people as those in my department.

Chapter 7

Though most people, my wife included, have always felt that I fit into the "How could anyone not like you?" mold, portrayed so perfectly in a popular Seinfeld episode, there have been a few students, and perhaps a teacher or two, over the years, who have not exactly found me to their tastes.

Late one afternoon, as I was attempting to unlock my car door in preparation for my long ride home, I found that the key was not making any progress into the lock. Apparently, something was preventing the little "trap door" that covers the keyhole from sliding open. Upon closer inspection, I found that the lock had been glued shut with a layer of clear super glue. I scooted around to the passenger side door, only to find it in precisely the same condition as the driver's side. The face of one of my students, a young boy in one of my morning classes, immediately appeared in front of my eyes, which by now were surely fiery red with rage. "Okay", I thought." "I'll just go in through the hatchback." Didn't happen! That lock had also been super glued. Storming back into school to find my principal, Bill Noble, I located him in his office and angrily explained what had happened to my car. Mr. Noble was a great guy, and he was genuinely concerned about my problem. He said that I should come see him first thing in the morning, and we would resolve the situation, to which I replied that I would certainly give him the chance to resolve it his way, but if that didn't work, I would resolve it my way. I didn't know what my way was, but I was not going to let this evil act go unpunished. Now that I had spoken with him, one little problem remained, how was I going to get into my car? Acetone! The substance found in nail polish remover! Yeah, that would do it, but where was I going to find some of that? A quick visit to the custodial office was the answer, and I was immediately given a large container of the glue-melting liquid, along with receiving multiple offers to assist me. It took me a half hour or so to dissolve the clear adhesive from the driver's side door lock, at which point I could finally insert the key and unlock the door. Not far from school was a well-stocked locksmith's shop, one which I had heard carried a full line of replacement auto locks of every description. With nothing to lose, I decided to stop by and ask if they had the locks I now needed for my two doors and hatchback. Incredibly, they had all three in stock, though the total cost exceeded $100.00. Armed with my new, glue-free hardware in hand, I made my way home, told my wife of my sticky little adventure, changed my clothes and got my tools, and hit the driveway to remove and replace all three locks. Two hours passed before I had finished the job, with door and hatchback interior panels having to be removed just to permit access to each lock. The repair brought out the seething jungle animal in me, with many wonderfully expressive words passing softly from my lips, fading into the early evening mist. No, that's far too poetic! I cursed like a sailor, like the New Yorker I still was, and I swore revenge upon the jerk, or jerks, who had perpetrated this crime.

The next morning, I stopped by Mr. Noble's office, with my bag of gluey goodies in hand. I detailed the entire incident, and the significant amount of time I had devoted to resolving it. He called in a few members of security, as well as the School Resource Officer, my friend and band mate, Hialeah police officer Carlos Llopis. Mr. Noble directed these good folks to "...get to the bottom of this." After thanking Mr. Noble, I walked with Carlos to his office, stating that I believed that I knew who the culprit, or culprits, could be. I was so sure of it! That young boy I mentioned before, the one from one of my morning classes, along with a couple of his "buds" from the same class, they had to be the ones who had done the deed. Carlos asked me for their names, and then told me to go start my teaching day and he would get with me later if he had information to share. Just before lunch, Carlos called me in my office, and asked me to stop by to see him ASAP. Peering through his office door from a distance, I saw three boys sitting next to his desk, heads bowed, and looking quite uncomfortable. Upon entering, Carlos asked one of the boys, the one whose face I kept seeing, to "...explain to Mr. Ringler what happened." "We don't like him." he said. They felt that I picked on them too much by asking them to answer questions during class, and by not allowing them to just sit quietly by while the clock ticked away the hour. So they had decided to get back at me by gluing my door locks shut. Wasn't that special of them? When asked by Carlos if I wanted to say anything to the boys, I said that I was amazed and disappointed that they would do something like that to me, and that I needed to have their parents come to school to discuss what had happened. They, and/or their parents, would also have to compensate me for my time and my $100.00, plus apologize to me in front of the principal. The three boys suddenly became my best friends, beseeching me to not call their parents, but I responded by saying that they had started the whole thing, and their parents had to know exactly what kind of kids they were raising. A few telephone calls were made, and before the day had ended, at least one parent of each boy was waiting for me in Carlos' office. After the dismissal bell had rung, liberating the masses, I made my way to meet with everyone in the Main Office. I had composed a document for each parent and student to sign, one in which the students admitted exactly what they had done to my car, and by which they and their parents agreed to compensate me for my time and repair expenses. Once signed by all parties, a copy of the document was placed in each student's permanent folder, and a copy given to each parent. A quick visit to Mr. Noble's office for an official apology, and to find out for how long he was going to suspend them, and the case was resolved. Upon returning from their forced five-day outdoor suspensions, I asked the boys to meet with me before lunch, which they begrudgingly agreed to do. I know I am far too forgiving of other's errors in judgment, I always have been and I always will be, but I wanted to let the boys know that as far as I was concerned the matter was a thing of the past. All I ever wanted was for them to participate and succeed, and if they hadn't understood that before the incident, they needed to understand it now. I asked them to please "raise their game" and start performing at a higher level. I didn't expect miracles, nor did I see any, but for the rest of the year, the attitudes of the boys seemed to change a bit, and they even began turning in their work. One of them even came to see me once in a while during the remainder of his time at HML, proudly sharing his report card grades with me and telling me how he was going to attend Miami-Dade Community College after graduation. The other two were probably just happy to be out my class when the year ended, hoping never to have to deal with me again. Hey, one out of three ain't bad. (I know, I'm not supposed to use "ain't", but...)

One late August morning, after summer school had ended and the new school year was but a week away, I received a telephone call from Bill Noble, my principal. Ray Harrell, it seemed, had decided to remain at the School for Advanced Studies. "What about the department chair position?" I asked. Mr. Noble's answer was direct and to the point: "You're the man, Mike." I asked him if he was sure that he wanted me to continue, and he was adamant about it. Suddenly I was faced with deciding if I indeed wanted to make the transition from interim to permanent department chair. For the sake of expediency, I told him that I accepted his offer, but during the next few days, I pondered my decision from every conceivable angle. Was I truly the guy to lead the department, or should I step aside and allow one of my more experienced colleagues to assume that role?

Every leader has an ego, though not every leader is egotistical. I've never felt myself to be the latter, choosing instead to be deferential and respectful of anyone I feel is more adept at something than I am. I do have every confidence, however, that my ideas and vision about leadership are for the most part on the money. I'm steadfast, sensible, and balanced. I consider both sides of every situation, searching for the one solution which will move people to action, yet not leave them feeling insulted or intimidated. From the many overwhelmingly supportive and positive comments I received from colleagues during my nineteen years as department chair of various departments, up until the day I retired, I believe I handled things the right way. Not everyone always agreed with me, but if I felt it best that a particular path be followed, that was the path that was followed. Of course, there were numerous occasions on which the administration made the decisions, sometimes pressured by district or state mandate, and choice was not part of the equation. At those moments, my task became one of convincing colleagues to get on board as quickly as possible, thus saving the energy they would otherwise have wasted by fighting a losing battle. Balance, the key is balance. On the day that my friend Lucy Felice retired, she came to see me while I was in the Media Center. Her voice shaking with emotion, she thanked me for always being a voice of reason, for always finding the middle ground that would satisfy the administration while protecting my teachers. Lucy understood, she always understood, and I loved her for that.

Chapter 8

Soon after the beginning of my second year as department chair, a tragic event took place which truly shook the very foundation of my world. On October 16, 1988, a teacher planning day, a student who had been with me as a tenth grader the year before, and whom I had just seen and spoken with that morning, was having yearbook pictures taken with her service club and club sponsor on the roof of our school. In those days, apparently, a number of clubs and organizations would have their group pictures taken up there. Later that day, while in my office with three of my teacher colleague friends, a loud crash was heard coming from the stairwell located just outside. Upon our investigation, we were horrified to see that a girl had apparently broken through a Plexiglas skylight designed to permit natural light to illuminate the stairwell, and had fallen approximately thirty feet or so to the stairwell landing below. The scene which lay before us was unimaginable and horrifying, a scene which remains emblazoned forever on my mind. A quick glance in her purse revealed the unthinkable to me; she was my former student from last year. How could this be possible? I had just spoken with her a few hours before. Jumping immediately into action, with students looking through the shattered skylight to the nightmare below, screaming in abject horror, two of my friends ran to my office to call the main office, one remained with the barely breathing girl, and I ran downstairs to find the principal. Emergency telephone calls were made, rescue vehicles sped to the school, and a rescue helicopter landed on the track area, directly adjacent to the school. Time had rarely moved so slowly for me before, but this moment was simply too unreal to play out in real time. With emergency personnel gathered in the stairwell, I stood with my friend, our arms upon each other's shoulders, trying to find the right way, some way, to deal with this surreal event. Upon returning home, I sat waiting for my wife to return with our young son who had been on a field trip that day. Upon their arrival, I explained to my wife what had happened, and immediately launched a steady stream of telephone calls to Jackson Memorial Hospital to determine the status of this young angel. Though at first the operator refused to provide me with any information as I was not a family member, I angrily insisted that she had been my student, that I was among the group of teachers who had first found her after her fall, and thus, I was indeed part of the family. This beautiful child had suffered massive injuries and was on life support, I was told. Calls placed throughout the night, every hour on the hour, brought the same response, until early the next morning, when I was informed that she had been removed from life support, and had quickly passed away. A heartbreakingly beautiful note about her life and about love, one that she had written shortly before her death, was printed alongside her photo in that year's yearbook. There wasn't a dry eye in the school for weeks to come. Many years passed before I was able to summon the strength to visit her grave, located in a lovely cemetery no more than a mile from our school. One day, as I was preparing to leave for home, I decided that was to be the day. I drove to the cemetery, parked my car near the majestic outside crypt in which she was interred, softly gathered together the few wildflowers I had picked near school, and walked slowly, ever so slowly, to the spot where she had so peacefully been resting since I had last seen her. I touched the metallic front of her crypt, laid the flowers into the small, attached, flower basket, and spoke to her. I told her how much I missed her, and how badly I had wanted to see her graduate, go to college, and grow into young womanhood. But, since I couldn't do any of those things, I just wanted her to know that I loved her, and that she would be in such a safe and special place in my heart that nothing could ever move her from there. I cried like a child, blew a kiss to her, and returned to my car for my long trip home. To this day, she is still safely inside my heart, and I think about her often. A wonderful photograph from the year that she was in my class sits upon a shelf in my bedroom, depicting me in full teaching mode, book in hand, looking directly at my gleefully smiling young angel, her eyes bright and clear and fully focused upon me. Her joyful expression, preserved forever in that photograph, is the face I will always see.

Chapter 9

At the end of the 1989-1990 school year, after I had completed three years as English Department Chair, my principal, Bill Noble retired. His replacement was to be Hal Blitman, then a middle school principal. Mr. Blitman had actually served as the head coach of the Miami Floridians, an old American Basketball Association team, for parts of the 1969 and 1970 seasons. He was introduced to me by Noble, who had brought him to my classroom. It was immediately clear to me that working for Mr. Blitman was not going to be like working for Mr. Noble. I did go to his office a month or so before the school year ended, in order to discuss a plan I had devised for the next year. At that time, a federal level lawsuit had resulted in new series of requirements for ESOL (English for Speakers of other Languages) students on a nationwide basis; the META Decree. States had to comply fully with all dictates of META, or face unspeakable horrors. As English Department Chair, I knew that there surely must be students in our school who would fall under the new guidelines, but there was no ESOL Department to handle their needs, that they had apparently always been placed in regular English classes. Therefore, I decided that it would best serve the interests of the school and those students if I were to create an ESOL Department, serve as its department chair, and ensure that the school was in full compliance with META on an ongoing basis. When I revealed my plan to Mr. Blitman, explaining that I planned to officially resign as English Department Chair that June, and assume the position of ESOL Department Chair for the following year, he told me that that decision had not yet been made. I told him that regardless of his decision, I was indeed going to resign as English Department Chair, and that if he did not want me to establish an ESOL Department and serve as its department chair, then I would gladly file transfer papers that day. I was going to stand by my decision no matter what, as it was clearly the correct thing to do for HML. He then asked me to sit down and explain the details of my plan for ESOL: how I would identify the students in our school who would need to become part of the new program, what other teachers might be willing to join me, etc. I shared whatever information I had been able to gather, including what I interpreted to be the basic dictates of the META Decree. Apparently, he was satisfied, and he said my plan was a "go". My four years as English Department Chair were coming to an end, and the magical, mystical world of META insanity was waiting for me on the other side of the summer.

Chapter 10

A single telephone call to my home early in the summer of 1991 instantly righted the listing HML ship, bringing news of monumental significance. Charline MacMillan, one of my English Department colleagues, contacted me to let me know that Mr. Blitman, our principal, had left HML for greener pastures in Houston, Texas, where he would be serving as an Associate, or Assistant, Superintendent of the Houston public school system. It seemed that our current superintendent, with whom Mr. Blitman was good friends, had accepted the superintendent position in Houston, and wanted Blitman to accompany him. I was stunned, but relieved. The thought of getting my new ESOL Department off the ground with Mr. Blitman around to oversee the process, did not exactly fill me with hope and positivity, but this news of his leaving for Houston invigorated me, and made me even more excited about my new role. When I had finished my conversation with Charline, and had hung up the telephone, I did actually whisper a "good luck" into the universe for Mr. Blitman. In some strange and unexplainable way, I almost liked that guy, and I really did wish him well.

Elliot Berman, the most wonderful principal with whom I would ever work, joined the HML family in time for the beginning of the 1991-1992 school year. He had been a successful middle school principal for the past few years, and we welcomed him with open arms. While I detected early on that he was less than fully comfortable in social situations, I soon recognized many of the other talents he had brought with him to our school. He was a powerful presence, respected by most, if not all, of the faculty and staff. His experience and prowess with the "nuts and bolts" of school operations was extensive, and throughout the twelve years he served with us as principal, our "house" was virtually always in order. The support he offered me as I began to implement my ESOL plan was unwavering. My leadership philosophy had essentially given me the opportunity to step beyond the officially designated duties of my previously held English Department Chair position, enabling me to become somewhat of a school-wide leader. Mr. Berman clearly recognized that, trusted me fully, and simply asked me to see him if I needed assistance with anything as I built the ESOL program. The ball was in my court, and the success or failure of my new ESOL program rested, as had the heavens supported by Atlas, upon my shoulders.

This new animal, ESOL, was as foreign to me as the English language was to my ESOL students. They spoke Spanish, Haitian-Creole, Urdu, a bit of Russian, and any number of other languages I didn't understand. How in the world would I move these kids, one hundred and fifty to start, eventually surpassing five hundred and thirty at the ESOL program's peak by the year 2000, to a level of English that would enable them to graduate, pursue college or other post-secondary educational paths, and ultimately become part of America's work force? How would I be able to comply with the rigorous dictates and record-keeping demands inherent within the META Decree? My initial staff of three teachers was totally behind me, as supportive of my efforts as was Mr. Berman. Whatever it would take, they were right there with me, dedicated to bringing to light all of my goals for our kids and the department.

Jeanne McGee, Linda Reisenfeld, and Belinda Smith. My ESOL pioneers! From nothingness, they helped me to fashion a new world, a safe world, in which scared and overwhelmed young kids whose old worlds had been left far behind, and who were expected to continue their education in a language they had only heard about, would now be able to comfortably begin the arduous task of securing their own piece of the American Dream. Imagine being suddenly transferred by your employer to a foreign country and being asked to immediately conduct business in a different language. Yes, of course, you would learn your new language as quickly as possible, so you say. But, the learning of a new language at the conversational, or survival level, is far different than mastering it at the academic level. The ability to ask someone where the library is, or to simply say "Good morning, Mr. Ringler", comes from a skill set of survival language that can effectively be mastered within a year or two. Being able to fully comprehend the subject matter of an academic text, regardless of the language in which the text is written, is known as academic language, a skill set which takes between five and seven years to acquire. A native, or fully fluent, English-speaking student reading a chapter in a history textbook does not have to fight the sequential battles of first struggling to translate every word into English, then trying to comprehend the overall meaning of the chapter. He or she simply reads the material and derives its meaning. The ESOL student, however, especially during the first few years in his or her new school, must initially translate the text of each chapter into his or her native language by searching word by word in a translator dictionary, or by utilizing an electronic translator device or, more recently, a cell phone "app". The result is usually a hit or miss jumble that requires an inordinate amount of time to construct, leaving very little room for true understanding. My philosophy concerning the acceleration of this process was clear, at least, I thought it was. I strongly urged my ESOL teachers, two of whom were fluent in Spanish, to completely refrain from conversing with our students in any language but English. Labeling every item in our classrooms with cardboard signs written in English was just the beginning. The concept of "modeling" was also heavily used. Starting with the most basic sentence forms, students were to utilize those structures as often as possible, in both their speaking and writing, substituting other nouns, verbs, and modifiers, for existing ones in order to create new sentences. Students were told to spend some time every night watching English speaking television programs. By surrounding them with English, my hope was that through the process of "immersion" they would get a jump start on this whole English "thing". It worked, at least in some cases. Within a few months, there were students who were having basic English conversations with their classmates and teachers, students who had bought into what was being sold in my department; a chance for success. It was frequently painful and uncomfortable, and took real courage on their part, but they began to see that it could work.

Chapter 11

Two short months before my new ESOL program was to take its first breath, the 1991 summer school session had just begun. I had taught summer school every year since coming to Hialeah-Miami Lakes Senior High School, and I was again fortunate to have secured a summer position. As my morning class moved along that first day, a young girl was already making quite an impression on me. Her hand was raised constantly, she volunteered to answer almost every question, she distributed and gathered materials, she simply could not do enough to help me. Sofia was her name, and she proudly told me that she was fourteen years old. Looking at her was like looking back in time. Her hair was done, as if she had used curlers or something, and she was wearing a dress, a DRESS !!! Every other girl was wearing pants and a t-shirt, and this girl was wearing a dress! All through the summer, she was among my best students. Every assignment was completed on time, she was respectful and intellectually curious; a teacher's dream student to be sure. At summer's end, she expressed to me that she was hoping with all of her heart that she would be with me again when the new school year started, as part of my new ESOL program. Well, she was with me again that year, and the year after that as well. However, during the first few months of her two year stint as my student, a darker side of her life was revealed to me. Clearly she was not a family favorite in a home filled with four boys, her stepfather's sons with her mother. Despite a photo that, she believed, captured a possible connection to the contrary, her real father appeared to remain unknown to her. She was treated like an outcast, someone who was in the way. There was very little money, even less food, and nothing but a bleak and lonely future ahead for her. I began to bring food to school for her. I left it in my office refrigerator so she could quietly pass by and take it without calling attention to herself. I made my teachers aware of her situation to avoid any embarrassment either on their part, or Sofia's.

Early in her sophomore year, just a few months after she had been with me in summer school, I was mentioning something about the animals at Miami Metro Zoo. She told me she had never been there, but hoped to go one day. After asking my wife that afternoon if she would like to have Sofia accompany us to the zoo sometime, to which she enthusiastically agreed, I decided to visit Sofia's apartment the next day to ask her parents for permission to have her join us that weekend. Thankfully, her parents were only too happy to give me their permission as they expressed their appreciation for my offer, and thanked me for coming to their apartment.

On the morning of our planned trip to the zoo, a smiling and enthusiastic Sofia was waiting for us at the front of her apartment complex. Here was a wonderful fifteen year old girl who had experienced so little joy in her young life, and if one simple trip to the zoo could fill her heart with a bit of hope and happiness, then I could only imagine how beautiful her life might have been had she been surrounded by a loving family, one in which she truly mattered. Bubbly and chatty as we drove to Metro Zoo, Sofia talked about any number of things that were on her mind, much of the time discussing "girl things" with my wife Rella as I sat quietly behind the wheel. (My wife believes that I am not capable of ever remaining quiet, so this brief episode of my sustained silence will likely have been forgotten by her.) Arriving at our destination a half hour or so later, Sofia made a beeline for the main entrance, a child about to enter a place that had only existed in her dreams, and as we passed through the tropical jungle-themed gates, she smiled a smile that came from deep down inside, a pure and precious smile that had been hidden for far too long.

Every area of Metro Zoo was a newly discovered treasure to Sofia. She gazed in wonder at the nearly century old tortoises; marveled at the mostly sleeping tigers, of both standard and white varieties; "oohed and aahed" at the giant, gentle gorillas, especially when viewing a tiny baby gorilla, nestled safely in the loving arms of its mother. Displaying a fiercely protective streak, she fought bravely to defend a stroller-riding young toddler from a minor swarm of nasty yellow jackets when we stopped for a bite to eat, and cheered mightily for the performing birds and other creatures that filled the metallic, open-air arena in which we sat on the last leg of our jungle journey before leaving for home.

As we pulled into the parking lot of Sofia's apartment complex, I knew that this day had indeed been a most special gift, for all of us. She hugged and kissed my wife, thanking her for sharing this adventure. I then escorted this soulful and courageous young girl back to her apartment, thanked her parents for allowing us to bring her along, hugged and kissed her goodbye, and returned to my car for the long trip back home. That day was to be the first moment of a lifelong, loving relationship with Sofia. Throughout the final two years of her time at HML, I remained Sofia's mentor and, in her far too generous words, her father. Along with my wife, I watched her on television when she sang on a famous Spanish-speaking variety show; gave her the money for her senior ring and senior pictures (after asking her parents if they would be comfortable with that); acted as mediator when, after graduation, she and her new husband were experiencing the myriad challenges faced by many young couples; and was at her side at the hospital a few years later, hours after the birth of her first son. Life has since taken Sofia down many pathways. She no longer lives in South Florida, but she remains inside my heart, a permanent part of my world. We speak every few months on the telephone, and bring each other up to date on "things": family, work, hopes, and dreams. She has visited our home since moving away, but such visits are rare, and difficult for her to arrange due to jobs, kids, distance, etc. Always a thinker and a ponderer, she has over the past few years found great solace by attending church. Not long ago, she called me at home to explain that when the clergyman at her church was discussing the joys of having a loving father, the only face she saw was mine. She told me that she loved me, and thanked me for always being there to support her; for teaching her the true meaning of unconditional love. I simply explained, as I had since we first met, that she was worth loving.

Dear Mr. Ringler,

I wanted to thank you for everything that you have done for me to make my life different and to make this world a better one for me. See all those messages around, there all for you cause that's how I really consider you. I know that I'm leaving school to start the real world but this is how it has to be even though I don't wanted leave school and leave my best teacher; and more than that a friend that has been like a father to me. Thanks for always been proud of me and not caring for those moments that I have fail. I hope God brings you all kind of blessing cause you really deserve it. You know that I'm not walking out of your life so easily, I will keep in touch with you and your family. My dreams are gonna come true because I have people like you in my life who make it better and believe in me like you.

Your stepdaughter (May I be?),

Sofia

Chapter 12

During my ESOL "period", 1991-2003, there was an endless stream of students from a variety of countries who entered, and subsequently left, my life. Kids from Cuba, Colombia, Venezuela, Dominican Republic, Nicaragua, Pakistan, Sweden, Russia, and numerous other points of origin, filled my department's classrooms every year. Some of them had been in the United States for a year or more, but a large percentage had recently arrived, taken from their original countries by parents looking for a better life. Regardless of how long they had been in the USA, however, fear was the constant companion of many of them. They were young, and afraid, and overwhelmed by the sudden demands placed upon them by having to learn a new language in an unfamiliar place. They came from middle class families, and from families that had nothing. Some traveled here on commercial airlines, and some risked their lives on small boats, or wooden rafts constructed of whatever materials could be gathered.

In 1992, at the age of seventeen, my future student Nizin decided to escape from Cuba in order to pursue his own American dream. He had discovered that his grandparents were Jewish, but had kept it secret as Cuban law prohibited the open practice of Judaism. Combining his desire to explore his Jewish heritage with his training as, and desire to become, an accomplished artist, Nizin knew that the only way he could truly complete himself was to relocate to the United States. Taking with him a few meager possessions, Nizin and his father traveled to the boat that was to take them, and a small number of other escapees, on a freedom ride to Florida. A few days into their treacherous journey, their boat began to take on water, and the entire group soon found themselves stranded on a small island near the Florida coast. For more than a week, they survived by drinking whatever rainwater they could capture, and by eating small snails they found scattered around their tiny island prison. They were finally rescued by members of the Bahamian Coast Guard, and placed in a Nassau jail until relatives in Florida were able to arrange for their release and delivery to the South Florida coastline, where they were subsequently rescued by the United States Coast Guard. Shortly after their arrival in South Florida, Nizin and his father, along with their fellow travelers, were granted political asylum

Once settled in the Hialeah area, Nizin was eventually enrolled as a student at HML, whereupon I was called in to determine his initial English proficiency level. During the brief evaluation I conducted for this purpose, I found Nizin to be fairly fluent in English, resulting in my placing him at the second highest level of ESOL classes. I had him entered into one of my classes, where he immediately began to progress at a much faster pace than did many of my other students. He was incredibly bright and perceptive, but what struck me most perhaps was his artistic talent. As I traveled between the rows of student desks, observing my students while they worked, I noticed that Nizin would always finish his assignments quickly, then turn his attention to a drawing tablet that never left his side. The doodles and sketches within were truly amazing! I was stunned by the quality. When I inquired about them, he simply explained that he had always loved to draw and paint, and his plan was to become an artist in the United States. With a deep attachment to heavy metal music, Nizin focused on creating album covers for many of his favorite bands, sharing them with me as he knew of my love for rock music in general.

One particular "Nizin" moment that remains so clearly in my mind was the day on which he presented me with a beautiful poster he had drawn, forever capturing a favorite saying of mine that he seemed to love: "There are two kinds of problems: the ones that life gives us, and the ones that we create for ourselves." It was an amazing piece of artwork, one which I proudly displayed in my classroom for many years thereafter. He told me that he would always remember me for my kindness and for my good advice, and I told him I would always remember his incredible talent and intellectual depth.

Since graduating from HML, I have neither seen nor heard again from Nizin, but I have recently discovered that he never strayed from his original dream of becoming an artist, or from openly pursuing his Jewish background. His incredible artwork graces the covers of a number of heavy metal albums, as well as being available in a variety of venues for all to see. It is likely that I will contact him in order to "fill in" the details of each of our lives, but whether or not that occurs, Nizin will always be one of the most unique and special kids I've had the pleasure of calling my student.

Chapter 13

Besides ushering in a new school year, August 1992 also brought with it the most devastating hurricane in recorded American history - Hurricane Andrew. This insanely powerful Category 5 storm, a wind event beyond all others, roared ferociously westward across South Florida, with winds obliterating nearly everything in their path. The destructive forces of Andrew were most intensely focused upon Miami-Dade County and points west, though Broward County certainly was hard hit as well. By the time the storm had departed, people had died, countless homes and other structures had been flattened beyond repair, and lives in general were changed forever. Peter Isquick, a teacher and good friend of mine at Hialeah-Miami Lakes Senior High School, called me to see how my family had done with the hurricane, and wondered if I wanted to travel down to school to see if we could assist in any way, as HML was a designated hurricane shelter. Just a week or so earlier, my wife and I had joined Peter and his wife Nancy at their home in Weston for an evening of music and singing, along with a few of their other close friends. Peter was a critically acclaimed opera singer, and Nancy had been a featured member of the Ice Capades in the 1970's. Ultimately, Peter and I each drove down to HML, but a day or two apart, and assisted in every way we could. Not long after Andrew, Peter called me to share some disheartening news; a melanoma which had been previously removed from his side, had returned with a vengeance, and was spreading quickly. Peter's father had succumbed to melanoma decades before, and it was clear that genetics were at work. Peter had the newly malignant melanoma surgically removed, a far more invasive procedure this time around, and left it at that, despite his doctor's insistence that he be further treated as deemed necessary at the Mayo Clinic or comparable medical institution. Being the free-spirited and holistic fellow he was, Peter chose instead to follow a course of "alternative" treatments to rid his body of any remaining remnants of the insidious invader, a choice which I was completely against from the start. Regardless of the weapon of choice, however, Peter became weaker and weaker, until he could no longer even speak to me on the telephone. Nancy and I spoke nearly every day. She was so hopeful that something would work, but that was not to be the case this time. One horrific day in December of 1992, Nancy called to tell me that Peter had passed away. I dropped to my knees and Nancy and I wept together over the telephone for a moment. Peter was such a pure and wonderful soul, and Nancy was cut from the exact same cloth. I told her that my wife and I were there for her in any way she might need. Per Peter's wishes, he was cremated and his ashes cast upon the waters of the Atlantic Ocean somewhere along the east coast of Florida. That was Peter; one with the universe and going his own way right up until the end. My wife and I attended a small gathering a few days later at Nancy's house, during which many wonderful stories of Peter and his life were shared by the attendees. When the time had come to say goodbye, I hugged Nancy as hard as I could, maybe so Peter would feel the love as well, then left with my wife to return home. I spoke with Nancy on a number of occasions after Peter's passing, but one call in particular almost literally knocked me off my feet. During the night, hours after we had lost Peter, I had a dream in which I clearly saw him walking towards me down the short hallway leading to my office. He smiled, but said nothing to me. He raised his hand, turned, and walked away. The very next day, Nancy called and asked if Peter had been in contact with me. Surprised by her question, I asked why she was inquiring about that. Her response was at the same time shocking and amazing. She said that a number of Peter's closest friends, all of whom lived in different parts of the United States, had called within a few hours to tell her of experiences similar to mine. She explained that Peter had "visited" his friends to let them "know" he was fine. Being an extremely spiritual and religious guy, I believe there to be some form of our "continuance" within the universe after we've passed away. Strange as it sounds, I've experienced it before and after Peter's death, with members of my own family. I'm not a nut, I swear! Yet, to hear that a group of people who were not in contact with each other had experienced virtually the same basic dream on one given night was a bit on the "uh oh" side of things. I told Nancy that I was amazed by her news, and after speaking with her a while longer, hung up the telephone, and relayed Nancy's news to my wife, her reaction mirroring my own.

Nancy remained in South Florida for a while longer before departing for Las Vegas. We spoke on a few occasions after that, but sadly lost contact as the years passed. Peter remained the subject of many lunchtime conversations with my colleagues at HML. He was talented and funny, quirky and unique, and most importantly, loved by everyone. Damn, I miss him!

Chapter 14

The beginning of the 1992-1993 school year found me facing new challenges for my ESOL program. It also brought to me another eager but frightened group of students in need of "Americanizing". One of the most amazing of these students was a young girl named Danmary. She was so quiet and overwhelmed that early on I was afraid she might not be able to move successfully through my program, but relying heavily upon my unlimited supply of patience and the ability to make kids believe in themselves, I began to see a difference in Danmary after only a few months. She still would shudder at the thought of responding in class, and would wave me off with a simple hand gesture, indicating that she had no intention of answering in front of her classmates. However, she would often stay for a moment or two after class, and softly whisper to me the answer I was seeking during class. A simple hug can work wonders with a child, it always has and it always will. Yes, I know that as teachers we were told to never touch a child, but that never worked for me. When a student would take that leap of faith and trust me, formerly a stranger, enough to hug me, there was no way that I was going to cringe in fear and withhold my affections from such a child. When I became a teacher, I swore to myself that I would treat my students as if they were my own children, and I hugged my own children all the time, just as my parents hugged me. I built an entire teaching career around letting my students know how much they meant to me, and hugging was a big part of that. Well, every time Danmary overcame her fear enough to answer a question, even after class, she knew exactly how proud of her I was. By the end of her tenth grade year with me, she had finally become comfortable enough to participate in class, and I felt that she had begun to scale the proverbial wall, on the other side of which lay her future success.

Continuing in my ESOL program for another year, Danmary virtually exploded academically during eleventh grade. Where in the world had this "new" girl been hiding? Her English improved exponentially, her grades began to soar, and she was rapidly leaving the other ESOL students far behind. She often came to talk with me before school, during lunch, and even after the day had ended, revealing her dreams; telling me that she finally felt like she truly had a chance to fulfill them. Her spectacular climb was the most powerful transformation I had ever seen in a student. A most willing audience, Danmary sought my advice and guidance in so many areas, putting so much trust in my responses that I felt as if I would be more at fault than she if her life didn't play out as she wished.

For her final year at HML, I moved her out of the ESOL program and into a regular English class. She had already begun taking advanced classes in other disciplines in eleventh grade, and expanded that as a senior. She still stopped by to talk with me as often as she could, and I cherished those moments as always, but I was even happier to see her so involved with school, spending time with her wonderful boyfriend, and just being a high school kid. It's an incredible feeling when a student with whom you've worked so closely actually gets to that special "place" you wanted her to reach. Success after success followed, and Danmary concluded her high school career with a substantial academic grade point average. The quiet and shy little girl who had first come to me as a tenth grader, newly arrived from Cuba, had now been reborn as a major academic force, one who was certain to continue her rise during college.

There were many tears shed on the day that she stopped by to write in my yearbook, and I in hers. Her words touched me so profoundly, and made me once again truly appreciate the power a teacher holds in his or her hands. We hugged each other, said our final goodbyes, at least until her graduation ceremony, and she left my classroom as my student for the last time.

After graduation, Danmary attended Florida International University, and to the best of my knowledge, subsequently obtained her Masters and Doctorate degrees from the same university. Back in 2006, a friend sent me a copy of a journal article containing information about a doctoral dissertation covering an incredibly advanced scientific process. I looked at the title, and as I glanced downward, much more out of curiosity than out of understanding, I caught the name of the author-it was Danmary! Not too bad for a child who had come to the United States as a non-English speaking child fourteen years ago. At the time, I could not find a way to contact Danmary to congratulate her, but recently (as in yesterday as I write this) I discovered that she had become a professor of engineering at a local college, and had gotten married as well. After an intensive internet search, I discovered that she had gotten married years ago, and of course, was now known by her married name. My attempts to reconnect with her were successful, and in a matter of a few days we were back in touch with each other via email. Incredible! After seventeen years, she brought me up to date on her family and her career in a single email. She was so excited to hear about my retirement, and related in detail a particular moment that had taken place in our class so many years before. I am of the belief that we all live within a "square", a comfort zone, and that every time we take a risk and do something that we are hesitant to try, our "square" grows a bit larger. Her life had been filled with many situations where she had put that philosophy into practice, thinking of the "square" and how she wanted to expand it as she moved along her academic and career paths. She had never forgotten that class moment, and was now in the process of introducing the concept to her own children. Happily, we have now planned for my wife and I to get together with her family in a month or so, and we will sit together and have one of our talks, just like when she was my student, except now she will have her husband and children beside her. Imagine how much we will have to share after so many years, including a warm and loving hug.

Mr. Ringler,

Can you believe it? I'm really leaving! I'm finally leaving! I can't believe three years have already gone by since I first entered the school. I can't believe I'm going to have to say goodbye to you, my guardian angel, and I won't see you again every day between classes, and I won't have the opportunity again to share all my great times, the bad ones, the sad ones, and the ones when I was in big trouble. There aren't enough words to express how much I've gotten to love you as a father, as a brother, as a friend, as a teacher. You've been there for me anytime, anywhere, all the time, ever since I met you, and back then you didn't even know me. Can you believe it?

Well, these 10 days left will go by flying, and even though it's hard for all of us to say goodbye, you've said that great things will come our way, and we'll be able to meet some other people (a lot more) and have a lot of different experiences as we all get into the world. You've said all that and I trust you, and I believe you. But I know I will never, ever again find someone like you.

I've been lucky enough to have known you for these years, and I know I'll never forget them, and I'll always come by to see you, to tell you about me as I've always done. And I'll come by to see you when I finish college, and when I get married, and when I have kids, and when they marry, 'cause I want you to share my important times because you are like a father to me. I'll always try to be strong as you told me to, and I'll try to reach only for the things that will positively affect my future.

This page will never have written everything I have to write because there really aren't enough words to express my gratitude for meeting you, and for all the help you've giving me, and for all you've taught me. Thank you. Please count me in as a friend of yours. Whenever you need someone, please give me a call. Keep on being yourself, that's the best you can be. See you until always.

Love you always,

Danmary

Chapter 15

With each passing year, the ESOL program grew larger and larger, serving more than five hundred students at its peak, one sixth of HML's population. Consequently, additional teachers were hired to join the department, with me always being asked to make the final "yea or nea" decision by Elliot Berman, my principal throughout my twelve-year ESOL "period". Of the twenty or so teachers who served with me at one point or another, the three stalwarts, the ones on whom I could always depend, were Jeanne McGee, Belinda Smith, and subsequently, Claudia Estrada. These ladies stood side by side with me, sharing my ESOL philosophy about putting the onus of learning English upon the young shoulders of our students. As a "gringo", I felt that the most productive environment in which our students would learn their new language would be one centered entirely around the use of *English only* in the classroom. Of course, this was always a difficult challenge when working with our newest students, the ones who had just arrived in the United States, but I felt it could be done through the use of modeling, and labeling, and total immersion. As I didn't speak any other language, my students had no choice but to respond to me in English, however limited their vocabulary, and for the most part over the years, it worked. Belinda, and years later, Claudia, were both Spanish speakers, but they always tried as best they could to refrain from using any language other than English during class. Jeanne was not a native Spanish speaker, but was fluent enough in it to communicate effectively with her students. Yet she almost never resorted to its use during class, urging her students to find the words in English, however long that took.

Unfortunately, after being with me for four or five years, Belinda had to leave HML. Her husband worked for the United States government in some capacity, and having just been promoted, was being transferred to his new position in Colombia, South America. Belinda came to me in tears on the day she found out. She was so upset about having to leave, but so excited about the new opportunity her husband, and similarly, her family, had been given. I thanked her for her incredible work over the years, and at the end of that year, she left. I heard years later that she and the family had returned to the United States, as a result of yet another promotion for her husband. One of the support staff at HML stopped me one morning to tell me that she had heard from Belinda, and that the first thing Belinda had asked was if I was still at HML. When told that I was indeed still a Trojan, Belinda smiled and told my colleague how much she enjoyed working with me and how much she missed me. As with so many other wonderful people I've met at HML, both students and teachers, I seem to have a knack for eventually tracking them down long after they've gone, so perhaps I will have an opportunity to get in touch with Belinda once again.

Jeanne McGee-my ESOL rock! For twelve years, this incredible woman stood by my side and supported everything I tried to do to assist our students, while concurrently doing all she could to help me fulfill the ever-changing and expanding onslaught of outrageous state and federal requirements forced upon schools by the META Decree. I never had to look over her shoulder, she was essentially *me*. I got to know her family, and watched her children grow, seeing them on the occasions when she brought them to school for teacher plan days. We shared thoughts and ideas, dreams and disappointments, and yes, we even disagreed once in a while, though we always managed to find common ground.

Jeanne's students adored her. They would come looking for "Ms. Mag-gee" every time they had a problem. As was the case with many of my students, they would come early to school to see her, spend their lunch period with her, and frequently stay after school to help her in her classroom. She was truly one of the most amazing teachers I've ever known.

Jeanne was a strongly spiritual and religious woman, well-schooled in the words of both the Old and New Testaments, and would frequently allocate a bit of quiet time for herself, just enough to read a verse or two from her ever-present, pocket-sized bible. She seemed to gain such strength from that, and we often discussed what she had read that day. It always struck me funny that, just as in the case with Graz and me, a Catholic and a Jew, a devout Christian like Jeanne and I could find so much common ground within our religious backgrounds. The clincher for me was that unlike so many people I've met who have based their belief systems upon extremely limited knowledge and understanding of their respective religious texts, Jeanne knew hers backwards and forwards, yet believed that the words of the bible could also be interpreted in different ways by the reader. Though she never seemed to doubt their authenticity, it always seemed to me that she felt that many of the stories contained within the Old and New Testaments could also be interpreted as metaphor, perhaps divinely inspired, but written by people as tools by which to guide, and possibly control, the masses.

In October 2000, when I had been nominated for "Teacher of the Year" for the third time, Jeanne came to me and insisted that I "play the game" and write an extensive resume to be used as the basis for voting by the faculty, rather than the brief, one-line statement that I had twice submitted after my two previous nominations. I explained to her that I never had been, and was still not, comfortable at all with the idea of selling myself to the faculty by presenting a "litany of wonderfulness" about myself, choosing instead to let the faculty vote for me if they felt so inclined. She disagreed with my decision, but said if that was the way I wanted to go, then she was behind me. At the next faculty meeting, the one during which the voting would take place, I was selected by the faculty as the "Teacher of the Year" for the 2000-2001 school year, apparently in spite of, or perhaps because of, my one-line statement. When I was told after the meeting that I had received 75% of the votes, even more meaningful when considering the two other incredible nominees, I was more than gratified that I had followed my heart by not going the "resume" route. After the meeting, Jeanne walked over to me and said that she had been wrong for doubting my decision, to which I replied that I knew she was just looking out for me and how much I appreciated that.

As the universe ebbs and flows like an oceanic tide, good things are often followed by less than happy events, and the conclusion of the 2000-2001 school year brought with it the end of Jeanne's tenure at HML. She came to talk with me one day, obviously troubled, and announced that she and her husband had decided to move from South Florida. Her news was difficult for me to hear. Jeanne was as much a part of the ESOL program as I was. She had been there from the start, and had helped me grow it into the living entity it had become over the past twelve years. How the hell would I be able to keep moving this *thing* along without her? We spoke for quite some time, and by the end of our conversation, I knew that she and her husband had made the right decision. Until the day eleven years later that I announced I was retiring, I just couldn't imagine how difficult it must have been for Jeanne to leave HML, but she knew it was time to go, and I fully supported her decision. The last day of school was pretty painful to say the least. I had ordered a keepsake clock for Jeanne, complete with engraved brass plaque, and presented it to her during lunch. She in turn gave me a limited edition John Lennon plate, which hangs on my living room wall to this day. One major disadvantage of remaining in a school for so many years is the development, and eventual ending, of so many wonderful relationships. I've always dreaded saying goodbye to my graduating students, and on that day, I absolutely hated saying goodbye to Jeanne.

Since leaving HML, Jeanne has been in contact with me a few times. I happily provided a letter of recommendation when she called to tell me that she had applied for a teaching position in her new town, and I was happy just to speak with her on the telephone for a few minutes. A few years later, she called to announce that she and the family were about to make another move, this time to California. I'd emailed her a few times with news of my musical "side-career", and she had always replied quickly. Lately, I have received no responses from her to my occasional emails, so God only knows where she is these days. Though I'll probably track her down, in case I am unsuccessful with that venture, at least I had the opportunity to work with her for twelve of my best years at HML.

Chapter 16

An obvious continuation of that group of special students who had made their way into my heart over the years, a wonderful young girl named Yasnay entered my program in 1997, ultimately graduating at the same time that Jeanne left our school in 2001. She was from Cuba, and like so many before her, she spoke little, if any, English. I recall her being with me for three years, growing into another highly successful student by the time I moved her from the ESOL program into Regular English for her senior year. She was such a sweet and sensitive girl, and I admired her for her dedication and excellent attitude about school. During our frequent conversations, I could see her great depth; this was no empty headed, destined for a low level career, student. Having Yasnay as my student for so many years was certainly one of the highlights of my career, but a couple of memorable moments stand among my favorite Yasnay stories.

When as a tenth grader she had started her second year with me, Yasnay apparently had made up her mind that she would get me to speak Spanish if it was the last thing she would do. My students all knew that I didn't speak Spanish, and I constantly reiterated that our classroom was a place for English to be spoken. Obviously, there were many students who could not fully adhere to my "rule", but better to aim high, I've always thought. As the months swiftly slid by, as they always do between the beginning of the year and Winter Break, Yasnay would badger me time and time again, pleading with me to say something, anything, in Spanish. That December, a few days before we were to leave for our two week vacation, Yasnay beseeched me to say "Feliz Navidad", but I refused. Over and over she asked me to say those two magic words, and over and over I would not comply. On one particular day, as her frustration level soared higher and higher, I said to her, "If you think I'm going to say Feliz Navidad, you're wrong." She continued to argue with me for a minute or two until it finally hit her - I had spoken Spanish! Unbelievably, she started to cry and buried her face in my shirt, sobbing and saying how she couldn't believe I had finally done that. I told her that it was my Christmas present to her, and that I hoped she was happy. On the occasions that we've communicated since her graduation from HML, I never fail to bring that story to light, just to let her know how much she meant to me as evidenced by my two word excursion into her native language.

A second, far more profound experience I had with Yasnay was during her senior year. She was no longer in my program, but like all of my students, was still part of the family. She was sitting with a friend in the hall outside my office one day, and when I asked her about possible career plans, she was unsure and directionless. I told her that I had always envisioned her as a nurse; that her sweet nature and caring attitude about other people would make her a prime candidate for such a worthwhile career. A day or two later, while reading my newspaper at home, I found an article which discussed the rapidly expanding growth of the nursing field in Florida, and the unmet need to fill all of the positions currently open, and yet to come within the next few years. I cut out the article, and gave it to Yasnay the next time I saw her. Something about the article struck a chord with her, and she soon informed me that she had decided to pursue a nursing career. I was so proud of her. After graduation, she entered the nursing program at Miami-Dade Community College, and upon completing the first two years of the nursing curriculum at that fine institution, she moved on to her final years at Florida International University. She was in touch with me a number of times while at Miami–Dade and F.I.U., sometimes just to touch base, and sometimes because she was overwhelmed by her coursework and simply needed a dose of Mr. Ringler. At those times, I would remind her of the day she walked into my class as a non-English speaking ninth grader, and how since that time she had succeeded at everything she had ever tried. I expected no different this time, I told her, and said everything I could to help her regain her confidence, and battle through the obstacles currently in her path. A reassuring hug always followed, and then she was off once again, moving steadily towards her goal. Upon graduating from F.I.U., Yasnay eventually secured a position in a home health care nursing capacity, which I believe she held for a few years until most recently securing a supervisory nursing position in a major South Florida hospital. When I contacted her to inform her of my retirement, she joyfully filled me in on the details of her new position, as well as some of the other wonderful things going on in her life. I told her that I knew all along that she was destined for great things, and she has proven me even more right every with every passing year. I miss Yasnay. I miss the times we had at HML, and the times when she would stop by while in college. I wish we could sit and talk once again, but that was always the hardest part for me as a teacher, letting go. I don't do that very well, despite people thinking that I do. It's impossible for me to just remove my students from my heart, to forget they were a part of my life. But as with so many of the kids I've cared most about, I know Yasnay is well prepared to face the challenges of her life. She is happy, highly educated, and secure career-wise, and that's what I wanted for her from the moment I met her, the very same things I wanted for my own children. I can't ask for more than that.

To my favorite teacher Mr.Ringler,

Mr. Ringler, it's so hard to say goodbye but I guess it's time for me to go. I want to thank you for being there for me all these years. I have enjoy so much being here in school because I always knew that you will be here whenever I needed you. Thank you for helping me with my English and with all my things; see now it's a great time because we communicate much better. To tell you the truth I always believed that you knew how to speak in Spanish. I want you always to remember me. I will be successful in life, and whenever I get my major, hopefully soon, I will come to visit you. What else can I say? You have been so nice and great to me. I think I wouldn't have been able to make it without your help.

I hope I see you at the graduation to say goodbye, not forever because I will come to the school just to see you. I will always remember you and all those nice things you did for me.

I wish you the best and may God bless you forever. Take care.

Love you,

Yasnay

Unlike Yasnay, who immediately demonstrated a desire to succeed in school, Fabiola seemed the polar opposite. When she entered my ESOL Program in 1997, I could clearly see how bright she was, but she seemed so distracted and unmotivated. No matter how much time I spent talking with her about the need for her to become more diligent about school, the more rebellious and distant she became. During the first few years she was in ESOL, her life had been a roller coaster of a few consecutive days in class, followed by suspensions for skipping and other misbehaviors. Consequently, she was always behind in her work, and her future prospects did not look good. Despite what my wife would say, I am a patient man. Being a teacher, however, required my level of patience to be ramped up considerably. In dealing with Fabiola, that ramp would have to be higher still. Looking for some connection with Fabiola that would enable me to reach her, I spoke with her about her voracious appetite for reading. Despite her failings as a student, she always had a book with her, often reading during class when other work was in need of completion. An English teacher's dream scenario! A kid who wants to read all of the time! In those situations, I would calmly approach her, to let her know that as much as I appreciated that she loved to read, there was work to be done first. The deal was that I would let her resume her reading once all of her work had been completed, a sequence that for the most part she followed. One particular day, Fabiola started frantically searching the area around her desk and began to cry. Upon questioning her as to the cause of her being so upset, she replied that a large sum of money was missing from her book bag. The money had been a birthday gift to her from a family member, and she was going to use it to buy a number of books she had wanted to read. Now, the money was gone, and those books would have to remain unread. My classroom contained a mini-library of high interest, teen oriented books, designed to accommodate readers at a wide range of reading levels. All through the year, I gave my students permission to peruse the collection, and if they found a book of interest, they could simply take it home to read it until completion. No sign-out sheets, just the honor system. The worst thing that could happen would be that a student kept a book that he or she had enjoyed reading, and I could easily forgive such a transgression. Fabiola had read nearly every book in that mini-library, and had planned to visit a bookstore in a nearby mall on the day her money had been taken. That plan was now shattered. There were other troubling parts of Fabiola's life that were hidden deep inside her, causing her to be far too sad for someone so young. What could I do to get her through this? The solution was clear. I would have Fabiola compile a list of the books she had wanted to purchase, buy those books for her, and present them to her as a birthday gift the next day before class. Seeking to keep my plan a secret from her, I simply asked Fabiola to write down the names of the books, telling her I would do what I could to see about "rounding up" a few of the titles. After school had ended that day, however, I drove directly to the Border's Books and Music store in Coral Springs, purchased the entire list of books, had them gift wrapped in one large box, and continued home, whereupon I explained the situation to my wife. The next day, before school had started, I found Fabiola in the hallway, and asked her to accompany me into my office. There, I gave her the birthday present, beautifully wrapped and crowned with a silky ribbon bow. Obviously stunned and confused, she asked me what was going on. "Open the package", I said. In the past, I had only seen Fabiola cry tears of sadness, and of emptiness. Her tears this time were tears of joy, glistening with the light of a child who has come to know that she is valued and worthwhile. She sat for a few minutes, looking lovingly at the covers of every book in the box. She asked me why I would do something like that for her, and I just told her how upset I had been to learn of the loss of her birthday money, and that I had no intention of letting her birthday pass by so unfulfilled. I told her that I believed in her, and wanted her to be happy. The connection had been made. Clinging tightly to me, Fabiola cried a bit, apologized for having gotten my shirt so wet, and asked if she could leave the gift in my office until the end of the day. A shy girl, one who did not like to draw attention to herself, Fabiola would pick up the books after school, hug me once more, and leave for home.

During her final year at HML, Fabiola was doing better in school, and making fewer and fewer errors in judgment, though one mid-year lapse led to her being withdrawn from school. She came to see me, embarrassed and ashamed of how she had let herself, and me, down. I knew that her withdrawal from HML would undoubtedly result in her not completing high school anytime soon, so I walked her down to the administrator who had just signed off on her withdrawal. I respectfully inquired as to the reason for this action, and when told that it was based upon Fabiola's resumed class cutting, I proposed a possible alternative solution. What if I were to carefully follow up on Fabiola's class attendance, and her grades as well? I would have her check in with me on a daily basis, and if I found anything to be out of order, I would contact her family, and the appropriate administrator, immediately. To my delight, my offer was accepted, and instead of being shipped out, Fabiola signed a "behavior contract", and was now obligated to perform or leave HML. Grateful for her one final chance to make it through, Fabiola did not let either of us down. She passed all of her classes, and graduated on time. A few years later, while in the middle of teaching a ninth grade class, I was contacted in my room over the PA system, letting me know that there was a delivery for me in the Main Office. After class, I hurried down to find out what had been left for me, and found a large "faux" flower arrangement, comprised of dozens of freshly baked cookies of all shapes and flavors, topped with a beautiful birthday card. "Happy Birthday, Mr. Ringler – With Love, Fabiola!"

Dear Mr. Ringler,

What can I say? I'm sorry about all of this. I screwed up AGAIN, but this time I guess I ran out of opportunities. I'm very ashamed with myself and I'm very sorry I disappointed you once again. You trusted me and I ended up skipping and getting myself in trouble. I don't know what to do or what to say. I did wanted to do better. I got good grades and studied for the HSCT and I passed it in the first try and now what? I just left all of that behind. I'm too brat and too wild and I'm sorry, I really am.

Fabiola

Chapter 17

By the time Jeanne left HML, the ESOL program had expanded to include a total of eight teachers, including me. I had basically "commandeered" an entire wing of the second floor for my use, with the full cooperation of principal Mr. Berman. Whatever I needed for the program, he was there to support me. What I needed most were teachers. The previous year saw a number of new teachers joining my department, and during the summer of 2001, Mr. Berman and I brought in a few more from within and outside the Miami-Dade County Public Schools system. I had a staff of teachers from a variety of backgrounds, but all were dedicated to helping the students in my program reach their full potential. Though a few others came and went, the core of teachers around whom the department thrived included Gloriela Blackmon, Vida DaCosta, Claudia Estrada, Nicolosa Jorge, and Olga Loperena, all of whom remained with me until I left the ESOL program in June 2003. However, the one teacher who stood tallest in my eyes was Claudia. The former ESOL Department Chair at Miami Springs Middle School, Claudia had a very clear understanding of what I was trying to accomplish via my program, and she backed me up at every turn. An excellent teacher, Claudia was outspoken and unafraid to share her opinions with me, a trait I welcomed and had always admired about Jeanne McGee. Clearly, Claudia was my new shining star, and I came to depend upon her much like I had Jeanne for so many years.

As she had previously been a colleague of some of my other teachers while at Miami Springs, Claudia seemed to welcome the opportunity to serve as an intermediary between my teachers and me. She made sure they knew what "Mike" wanted, even after I had made it more than clear, often spending her lunch period eating with the others in my office. The others looked up to Claudia, and they recognized that she was firmly behind me, expecting them to do the same. For the remaining two years that I was with the ESOL program, Claudia most assuredly made my job a bit easier.

The department flourished, with a reputation for excellence and high standards that continued to spread throughout the school. Many of our students started at point zero, with little or no English, but were willing to lay everything on the line in an effort to succeed. If they were embarrassed to participate in class, they kept that to themselves and volunteered anyway. As they moved through the program, they began to see the results of their own diligence, and that in turn provided them with the courage to continue. As I look back on the endless stream of students who passed through my program on their way to young adulthood, I am so proud of those who graduated on time, and continued their education at the college level, or via other options such as vocational schools or the military. I still hear from some of them even today, filling me in on all of the wonderful details of their successful lives, and thanking me for being there to get the whole thing started so many years before. ESOL students are a unique breed. They come from places far and wide, leave friends and their world behind in order to learn English, and primarily set their sights on helping their families financially in return. For the most part, they have a deeper appreciation, much of which originates from their family, for the opportunities which lay ahead of them in the United States. They often initially hide behind their native tongue, more out of fear than anything else, and frequently take a great deal of time to get "going". But once they begin to taste the success that their own hard work brings, they feel empowered enough to push onward.

Before the 2002-2003 school year came to a close, I decided that at age fifty I had had enough of the META Decree, and the endless hours of paperwork and documentation that it required in order to be fully compliant. For twelve years I had spent far too many late afternoons and evenings in my office, updating more than five hundred student folders and writing reports, all in preparation for the inevitable district and state ESOL audits that were sure to come. I thought I knew what to expect when I first started the program twelve years before, but the governmental requirements simply spiraled out of control. It felt like the time was right for me to step away from my ESOL program, and turn the reins over to someone else. The need for me to do so had become increasingly evident every time I attended district ESOL meetings, at which one of my favorite assistant principals, Marteen Longo, would frequently join me. As we drove to each meeting venue, she would always ask me to please refrain from getting into trouble by speaking out when I disagreed with whatever was being espoused by the powers that be. I told her that I just couldn't do that; if these people are wrong they need to know about it. When district directors and supervisory staff are presenting information that is inaccurate and misleading, and will ultimately cause innocent, well-intentioned ESOL employees to be admonished for doing what they had incorrectly been instructed to do, I had no choice but to bring their errors to light. I certainly did not make many friends among the higher-ups, but that was of no concern to me. The people who mattered were my ESOL counterparts: department chairs and teachers and paraprofessionals who would undoubtedly pay the price for the failings of our supposed educational leaders. Only two years earlier, the district ESOL Supervisor visited me one day that year to advise me that her position was being split into two positions, with a separate supervisor for both the north and south areas of the county. When she asked me if I would be interested in the north area position, I immediately replied in the negative. I had no intention of "playing the game". I would not last five minutes I told her, as I would be certain to open my mouth to whomever I needed, whenever I needed, and that my new bosses would definitely not appreciate such behavior. I could best serve ESOL students by being their teacher, by running the department, and by continuing to be a voice of reason against the foolishness being continually thrust upon ESOL folks by district and state officials who knew virtually nothing about education and kids. That I had dutifully done for the next two years, but now I had decided to inform my soon-to-be-retiring principal Elliot Berman that I was going to step down as ESOL department chair when the school year ended. When asked what I wanted to do next, I told him that I thought I could turn the CSI, or Center for Specialized Instruction, into a true learning center, rather than a holding area for misbehaving students. All sorts of ideas came to me about how to equip the CSI room with computers and educational materials. Always one of my biggest supporters, Mr. Berman wholeheartedly agreed with me, and said it was a go. I then called a meeting with my department to advise them of my decision. I told them that I would be recommending Claudia Estrada as my replacement, and that seemed to assuage any fears of some outside entity stepping into their territory and changing things for the sake of change. At first, Claudia was unsure about assuming my position, but if I'm anything, I'm a motivator, and it wasn't long before she acquiesced. After twelve years, I was about to take another step forward, or so I thought.

Chapter 18

Our principal, Elliot Berman, retired from Miami-Dade County Public Schools after twelve years at HML and probably twenty-five to thirty more during his pre-HML career. He was a great principal, and became a friend to me as well. When I first met him, I felt that he was rather shy for a man in such a visible position, but found, in time, that reserved was perhaps a better description. He came to us from Ruben Dario Middle School, where he had been principal for a number of years. Everyone there loved him, and it wasn't long before that same feeling spread throughout the HML community. Of course, there will probably never be a principal whom everyone loves, but Mr. Berman came pretty close. Things were different back then, with FCAT just starting to rear its ugly head, and the spirit of the "old days" at HML still floating through the hallways. Mr. Berman arrived at HML the same year as I was starting the new ESOL program, and as I mention elsewhere in the book, he was a great supporter of ESOL and of my efforts to take care of HML's ESOL population. He seemed to be incredibly proficient in so many areas, and there was certainly nobody more adept at keeping our financial "house" in order over the years than Mr. Berman.

Every year, a few weeks before the Jewish High Holidays of Rosh Hashanah and Yom Kippur, Mr. Berman would call me down to his office and ask me to go over the list of faculty members with him in order to try and identify who was Jewish. Then he would sign and deliver to their mailboxes Jewish New Year's cards. I always found that to be very nice touch from a real "mensch", a good guy! One day he sat me down and divulged the entire history of how his family came to be so well known and respected in Cooperstown, New York. Yes, *that* Cooperstown, home of the Major League Baseball Hall Of Fame. If I remember his story correctly, and I'm sure I'll be wrong on some of the details, when Mr. Berman was a child, there was a reasonably sized Jewish population already established in that area, many of whom kept kosher homes, but there was no kosher bakery anywhere near Cooperstown at which they could purchase kosher breads and other baked goods. Thus, his grandparents had an idea: why not drive down to New York City once a week, fill their car with baked goods from one or more of the many kosher bakeries there, and bring everything back to Cooperstown to sell to the local Jewish folks. Needless to say, the idea virtually exploded, with bread flying out of the car (figuratively, just figuratively) faster than it could be transported into town. From that point, faced with such a huge demand for kosher baked goods, and with driving back and forth to New York City being so time consuming and stressful, Mr. Berman's grandparents started their own kosher bakery in Cooperstown, and the rest as they say, is history. (Unless of course my facts are somewhat skewed, in which case the rest as they say, is wrong.) The Berman family grew in stature within the Cooperstown community, and even had a street named after them. I suppose the pressures of bakery related fame grew to be too much for Mr. Berman, as he eventually relocated to the Miami area.

Mr. Berman always tried to get me to call him Elliot, which I took as a wonderfully respectful compliment. For some reason, however, I just was never comfortable doing so, and continued to call him Mr. Berman. I had never thought of calling Mr. Noble by his first name, believing that his age and years of experience had made him deserving of being called Mr. Noble. Though I felt closer to Mr. Berman, and he insisted it would be fine if I did so, it was still a similar situation to Mr. Noble's. Mr. Berman was...Mr. Berman! Yes, I was only about fifteen or sixteen years his junior; yes we were connected through our Jewish backgrounds; and yes, he had invited me to call him Elliot; but it just didn't feel right. With all of my principals after Mr. Berman, I've called them by their first names: Richard, Karen, Chris, and Jose. I was older than three of them, and only a couple of years younger than one, so it felt appropriate. Perhaps as I aged, and had become one of the truly well-established members of HML's "old guard", I felt that I had earned the right to call these good people by their first names.

When that moment came on the very last day of school, the moment when Mr. Berman would retire and walk away from HML, he stopped me in the hall and asked me to go with him to his office. The timing was perfect, as I had brought with me that day a beautiful wooden clock I had purchased, featuring a brass plaque inscribed with my personal thank you to him. I went to my office to retrieve the gift, and when I returned to his office, I asked him to open it. He became a bit teary-eyed upon reading the inscription, and thanked me for having thought of him. He kind of bear-hugged me, and said how much he had always appreciated my friendship, my loyalty, and my strong leadership within the school. I don't do goodbyes very well, though I've gotten better at them over the years. Once someone has been a part of my life, they are supposed to remain in my life forever, but that rarely, if ever, actually happens. He then started going through a few boxes which were scattered around his office, taking out and handing to me a new HML windbreaker here, and an HML baseball cap there, along with a few other HML mementos, all of which he wanted me to have. I thanked him for his generosity, told him I would be I touch after he had moved to Atlanta and settled in, then turned and walked out of his office for the last time.

With Mr. Berman being Mr. Berman, his retirement did not go exactly as planned once he had settled into his new life in the Atlanta area. With his incredible reputation preceding him, he was quickly hired as a teacher and part-time assistant principal in a neighboring county, hired by none other than a former Miami-Dade County Public Schools superintendent, Frank Petruzielo, and the man who had been his assistant/associate superintendent in Houston Texas, our own former principal, Hal Blitman. By the next year, Mr. Berman was placed as the principal of a large high school in the county, where he remained until accepting the principal position at a brand new high school a bit closer to his home. Though I haven't spoken to him in quite some time, the word on the street has it that he served in that position up until only a year or two ago, when he re-retired. God only knows what he's up to these days, but I hope whatever he's doing, he's happy.

Chapter 19

How strange it would be to run an instructional program via CSI. A department chair no longer, and with no traditional English classes to teach, I wondered how to make this new idea of mine work at the same level as my previous programs. Unfortunately, no sooner had Mr. Berman retired, then our new principal, Richard Vidal, stepped in and nixed my move to CSI. With his eye on returning HML to its former glory as a major athletic force within the county, he wished to bring back a highly touted coach who had run a highly successful track team at our school a few years before. In order to do that, he had to have a spot to which he could assign that individual. CSI would be it, and I was quickly out of the picture and in need of a position within the school. I wasn't angry at Richard, in fact, I grew to like him very much during the six months he remained as our principal, and years later when he had become a regional director with HML under his jurisdiction. During a conversation I had with assistant principal Marteen Longo immediately after Mr. Vidal had informed me of his CSI decision, she expressed her dismay over what had transpired and asked me what I wanted to do. I inquired as to the availability of ninth grade English classes as I had always felt that the youngest kids needed the strongest teachers, and when told there were plenty of ninth grade sections available, I asked her to give me six of those classes. She did a bit of a double-take, as very rarely did anyone intentionally seek assignment to ninth grade, but I insisted that was what I wanted for the next year. We ran the idea past Richard, who was happy to have that problem solved so easily, and thus, after having been away from the English Department for twelve years, I was to return after the summer once again.

The summer passed uneventfully, and it was time to return to the classroom and get my new charges moving. It certainly felt unusual not being the one making decisions about the running of a department, but I would have to get used to that. Graz, my closest confidante', shared with me that it didn't matter if I held the position of department chair or not, I was still a department chair in my head, and the rest of the school still held me at the highest possible level either way. That sounded about right to me. I could still have a voice in the running of the school, just not the authority on paper to do anything about anything. It never mattered if was actually in charge, I just chose to conduct myself as if I were.

I absolutely loved my ninth grade classes. We read and discussed literature, focused upon improving writing skills, talked about life; all the things I had always done with my students. I met some of the most wonderful kids in those classes over the next six years, the total time in which I taught ninth grade. One of the highlights of each of those years was the teaching of *To Kill A Mockingbird* by Harper Lee. That had always been among my favorite books, and like millions of other readers, I had found it to be one of the most life-changing books I had ever read. The quiet heroic power of Atticus Finch brought a lump to my throat and tears to my eyes, even in class, and I occasionally had to stop to regroup as I read selected sections aloud to my classes. It was not at all uncommon for my kids to yell out during the reading of the book, especially when hearing of the gross mistreatment of Tom, and the sneaky and cowardly racially charged viciousness of Bob Ewell. By the time each class had finished reading the book, six years in a row, there were students who voiced their opinion that it was the best book they had ever read in their lives. For many of them, it was one of the *only* books they had ever read in their lives, at least prior to coming to my class, but I understood, and I knew how deeply they had been affected by the book.

One of the things I loved most about my ninth graders was their high level of gullibility. I know I can be very convincing when I speak, and many adults have fallen under my "spell" and bought into the stories I've created right under their noses. But ninth graders, they believed everything I told them. It was almost too easy. My favorite, and the favorite of many of them, was the story I devised to explain a tiny piece of knitting yarn I had installed up by one of my classroom's air conditioning vents. When each year started, inevitably there would one kid who would ask what the string was for. With the most serious face I could muster, I scientifically explained that the string was actually an "air indicator", which I had carefully designed after months of trial and error. The string was exactly the right length and exactly the right weight to move properly when the air conditioning was blowing correctly. Sometimes, they would spend minutes just staring at the quivering wooly appendage, pondering the effort it must have taken to design such an instrument. I could keep up my charade for months, and for the most part, they believed it. Of course, eventually I would rat myself out and explain how I had been kidding all along. Goodness, some of them actually seemed disappointed to find out that in reality I wasn't a scientific genius.

As if the universe knew how much I wanted to be in charge of *something,* one day Richard called me into his office and said that in May 2005 HML would be going through its next five-year SACS (Southern Association of College and Schools) accreditation visitation, and that he wanted me to join him, and a few other HML staff members, at the upcoming SACS Convention in Tampa. This event was far more of an intense, two day, training session designed to assist schools with their upcoming SACS evaluations, than a standard convention. In the afternoon of the second day, one of the assistant principals who was attending the convention with us whispered to me that Richard was going to talk to me when the day's festivities were completed. As it turned out, Richard had asked Mr. Berman just before he departed for the name of the person who would be able to motivate, direct, and supervise the entire faculty and staff for the next two years, leading and guiding them towards the goal of continued accreditation, and Mr. Berman had told him that I was the one he needed to put in charge.

Despite the realization that this position would require untold hours of extra work on my part for nearly two years, I accepted Richard's request that I become HML's SACS Chairperson. As the devil is always in the details, I'll let the devil take his details elsewhere while I cut to the chase. Every leadership skill I had ever thought I'd possessed was called into play during the preparation period leading up to the May 2005 SACS Evaluation Team visitation. I had to organize, motivate, and guide the entire HML staff: faculty, administrators, custodians, cafeteria workers, security monitors, et al; into an army of SACS-crazed soldiers. Everything we did was SACS, SACS, and more SACS. I set up committees to handle each evaluation component, assigned chairpersons and co-chairpersons for each, devised a meeting schedule, visited each committee during every meeting, and proofread and revised every document produced by every committee before eventually utilizing every bit of research to produce an eighty page report, copies of which needed to be sent to the SACS folks a few months in advance of their visit. In general, I became one giant pain in the butt to a large number of people, though according to those who would still talk to me (just kidding), everyone felt comfortable with, and supported by, me through the entire process.

Sometime in April 2004, after having been with us for only seven months, it was announced that Mr. Richard Vidal, our principal, had been reassigned to a position at the Region office, and that Ms. Karen Robinson from Lawton Chiles Middle School would be replacing him. The process was completed in short order, and Karen (I told you that I now felt comfortable calling my principals by their first name, didn't I?) stopped by HML in order to be introduced prior to taking up residence with us within a week or two. No sooner had she finished her "happy to be here" speech, then she sought me out and asked me about our SACS Evaluation status. We now had only a bit more than a year left in which to complete everything, and she needed to know exactly where we were. I filled her in on our progress to date, and she seemed more than relieved to see how far we had come.

Karen's first full year at HML found me in the midst of a SACS whirlwind, with a number of secretarial staff members being assigned to type as quickly as I could finalize each bit of research or report component. The required SACS components were being addressed and analyzed right on schedule, and before long, hotel arrangements were being made for the ten person visiting team, along with preparations for the first evening's SACS banquet and introductory meeting, a practice that has since fallen by the wayside, rightfully so, due to the sheer expense of it all. The entire school population was well aware of what was about to transpire in early May that year, and on the first day of the three day visit, the pieces smoothly fell into place, one after the other. I had never heard my name called over the PA system so often as I did during that seventy-two hour period. "Mr. Ringler this" and "Mr. Ringler that". I know, I asked for it when called upon to take charge of the process, but it had become overkill at this point, and I just wanted it to be completed, which it soon was. The visiting team included in their report many outstanding commendations about our school, as well as a few well-intentioned recommendations which we were urged to address over the next five years in preparation for our next SACS visit, in 2010. The team's report was presented to the entire faculty and staff at an long faculty meeting on the final afternoon of their stay, and when they announced that they were indeed recommending HML for another five-year continuation of our accreditation, my friend Tony D., with whom I was sitting, quietly fist bumped me and said, "Mikey, you did it!"

Karen was obviously relieved as well, and as the meeting ended and people began exiting the Media Center, she came over to thank me. We hugged and took a few deep breaths together, both agreeing that we would soon sit down with other staff members to look into the implementation of the SACS visiting team's recommendations, something we actually did at the beginning of the next school year. At our end of the year luncheon in June, Karen presented me with a lovely commemorative plaque on which was inscribed a brief, but meaningful, message about leadership. Though I certainly received my share of them during my career, plaques and other physical awards were never my focus as a teacher and department chair, but I always appreciated it when someone took the time to offer thanks for a job well done. I do have a well-defined philosophy when it comes to leadership, and the few words which were carefully etched into the brass plate of the plaque reflected a small, but significant, component of that philosophy.

Karen Robinson remained HML's principal until the conclusion of the 2007-2008 school year. During her tenure, HML continued to be mired in an FCAT "funk", with our Florida school report card grade remaining primarily a "D", though we did enter "F" territory one time, immediately after our inclusion in the failed "School Improvement Zone" which I've previously discussed. This school report card grade monster, based almost exclusively upon FCAT scores, was simply the wrong tool by which to measure a school's success. To this day FCAT still remains a failure, and as discussed earlier, the revised school report card grading system is so flawed that even the state does not know how to properly utilize data to properly calculate school grades. In July 2012, after recalculating school report card grades at the elementary and middle school levels due to having incorrectly calculating them initially, more than a hundred schools found their grades increased by at least one full letter grade. My God, if the state that devised the system cannot figure out how to correctly determine its schools' grades, exactly how legitimate can the results truly be, and how can they be used as a measurement of a school's "success"? It's so blatantly a case of people who know very little, if anything, about education, arbitrarily devising pathways by which to lead schools to the promised land as measured by the least effective and least reliable means by which to measure true learning – standardized tests.

Despite Karen's dedicated efforts, HML did not improve, at least on paper, and she was reassigned as the principal of John F. Kennedy Middle School for the next year, 2008-2009. She had tried so hard to put HML back on track, but the odds were against her, as they would have been for anyone, and the district will only be patient for a limited time, so away she went. She was above all, a caring and compassionate person, and a good principal to boot, but to the district, that doesn't translate into a "B" grade, so off she went. I missed her bubbly enthusiasm, and the conversations we used to have about music and family, and her desire to make HML the great school it once was, but I'm happy at least that she found a new home at Kennedy. I'm willing to bet that the good folks there were just as happy to have her as their principal.

Chapter 20

When I assessed each of the six years I taught ninth grade, I firmly believed I had made a difference. As my career unfolded, I always believed I made a difference, but I somehow could see it more immediately with the little ones. They seemed to be ready to go fully in one direction or the other, and if caught at precisely the right moment, they could be placed upon the more positive path. With the beginning of each new school year, I found myself staring at six classes of slightly older middle school babies, but by the end of each year they had begun to mature, ever so slightly, into "almost" high school students. Some of those kids turned out to be among the closest to me of all of my students, with many of them from my final ninth grade group remaining with me as they moved to tenth grade, where they discovered that I had done the same.

One of the ninth grade students who I had with me for just one year, but who connected with me right from the start was Joseph. Intelligent, inquisitive, and tremendously verbal, he proved quickly to be a top flight student with unlimited potential. He was a nice boy, raised by a loving mother and closely bonded to his aunt. He was polite and courteous, and almost always addressed me as "sir", something most of my students would never think of doing. His plans for the future were unclear at that time, but would ultimately move him in the direction of a teaching career. As much into music as I was, when we weren't discussing literature he would pepper me with questions about my favorite bands, their best albums, what instruments I played, and my earliest recordings. When an early song of mine was to be played on the radio in Italy, and the station had apprised me of the time it was going to be streamed live over the internet, Joseph was there to hear it. He found it hard to believe that I was actually on the radio, in Italy no less, and that seemed to cement our musical relationship even more firmly. Until the day he graduated, and long after when he was a few years into his college education, music was the first area he wanted to discuss whenever we were in touch.

Having now completed more than half of his college credits as he pursues his degree in English, including many of his required Education courses, Joseph appears to be well on his way towards becoming an English teacher. If and when that takes place, and he stands before his first group of students, they will be in for a treat. He will be a wonderful teacher, and he will fill his students' heads with tales of his high school education long ago, and his love of music, and perhaps some young kid will step forward one day and say "Excuse me, sir." Tick-tock, tick-tock.

Of all of the beautiful kids who were with me as ninth graders, there were a number of them who quickly took up permanent residence inside my heart, where they remain to this day. When I accepted the position as Language Arts Department Chair for the second time in 2009-2010, my administration and I felt it best for me to teach tenth grade classes, the group for whom the FCAT was most critical. In doing so, a number of my ninth grade students found themselves with me for another year of English. Most were excited to be there, though a few low achievers would surely have preferred to be with another teacher. I expected too much of them, and held them to high standards, and they had seen enough of that from me during the last year. In general, however, most of my students welcomed the chance to join me for another go round. As teachers, we most often enjoy the company of our students for a single year, getting to know them as much as we can in that relatively short period of time. When given the rare opportunity to spend an additional year with them, well, that's where relationships, some that may last a lifetime, are forged. That clearly took place during my first year in the tenth grade.

Stephanie was a tiny little ninth grader, dark haired and dark-eyed, and as smart as they come. While with me for English I Honors, "Steffi" proved to be incredibly perceptive, self-motivated, and mature beyond her years. She was outspoken, had some good friends in the class, and loved to discuss matters pertaining to both school and the world outside. By the end of ninth grade we had become closer, though I always felt that I didn't really know her yet. It was upon discovering that she was to be with me again for tenth grade, and during the time that she remained at our school, that she revealed more of the "complete" Stephanie to me. She wanted to study photography. Her dad was a photographer, and as a neighboring high school offered a fairly extensive program in photography, she was going to transfer to that school, sometime during the year. I was so excited for her, despite knowing I was soon to lose one of my most special kids. I hated losing my kids. They were part of my world, and when they left, my world became a bit emptier, and a bit dimmer. Stephanie's stoic and mature perspective about her impending move was admirable. She knew what she wanted, and she was going to pursue it. When her final day arrived, all of the emotions she had kept so carefully hidden inside found their way into the light of day, and she softly wept while holding her friends, and me, oh so tightly. Then the bell rang, and she was gone. Another of my students, Karen, kept in touch with Steffi after her departure from HML, reporting to me with updates whenever something new needed to be shared. Upon becoming a senior, Steffi began to correspond with me via email. Some changes in her plan had taken place, and she was now in yet another school, but she was always about moving forward, and that was the picture with which she presented me. Steffi was so excited about her upcoming graduation, and what was to follow. Once I had retired and she had left high school behind, she told me of some changes in her life and in her college plans, at least for the immediate future. With the same stoic nature, she revealed to me her changing circumstances, and her plans to make the best of things nevertheless. They were good plans, forward thinking and well thought out. We have communicated many times this summer, the summer of her graduation and of my retirement, and I have complete and total confidence that Stephanie will find the success she has sought for so many years.

Eadivah; what to say about Eadivah? She was the younger sister of another HML student, and was now a ninth grader in my English I Honors program. She was one of the good kids, the kind who immediately find their way inside a person's heart. With a cheerful disposition and a sunny smile on her face almost all of the time, one just couldn't be sad around her. Eadivah worked hard and never missed class. Her work was always in on time, and her hand was always in the air, a signal to me that she had something to share. I've rarely known students who have possessed such an unfailing, innate sense of right and wrong, clearly a result of the extensive time and effort committed to her by her parents. How excited I was when I moved to the tenth grade the next year, only to find her name on the roster of one of my classes. We would be spending another year together, and this extra time strengthened the bond we had already shared. Eadivah became more confident and comfortable during her second year with me, even assuming an "almost" leadership role in class when she decided the students were in need of being "reined in". One facet about our relationship that I found most intriguing was the fact that she was of Palestinian origin, I was Jewish, and shockingly, we cared very much about each other and got along beautifully. I distinctly remember a discussion she and I were having in class, one in which she said that she had been talking about me with her family. "They know I'm Jewish, right?" I asked. She replied in the affirmative, stating that that was not an issue for her family, to which I responded, "We should be on a poster together, hanging somewhere in the West Bank, just to show everyone on both sides of the Middle East conflict that it can be done. Imagine, a Palestinian and a Jew, able to co-exist and maintain a warm and loving relationship. What a concept!

For her remaining two years at HML until graduation, especially after she had become a teacher aide, Eadivah was a frequent visitor to my classroom: before classes, just prior to lunch, during my planning periods, the day before major holiday breaks, etc. She passed by as often as possible to say hello as I stood in my traditional between-class position in the hallway in front of my classroom. When the time had come for her to graduate and move on to college, Eadivah spent even more time with me than usual, knowing that she would soon be leaving. Graduation came and went, but Eadivah began sending me emails almost immediately. We have continued to correspond in that fashion throughout the summer of 2012, and I have no doubt that we will always be in touch on a regular basis.

A bookworm! That's what Amanda would have been called when I was in high school. She read all of the time, it was apparently her favorite activity. When she received money as a birthday gift, and I asked her what she planned to do with it, she replied "Buy books."

Amanda was one of my prize ninth graders in 2008-2009. Quiet and unassuming, she came to class better prepared than almost anybody else, participated in every discussion, wrote at a near college level, and essentially mastered everything I could throw at the class. Upon meeting her mother at Open House that year, and finding her to be one of the most dedicated and supportive parents I'd ever met, it was easy to see why Amanda had become the superior student she was. As a sophomore, she was one of the students who moved along with me to English II Honors, and our second year together gave me the chance to see even more of the real Amanda. I don't know if it was simply that she had grown a year older, or that she simply felt more comfortable the second time around, but she revealed aspects of herself that I hadn't seen much of the year before: a somewhat sillier-than-expected sense of humor, a more sociable nature with classmates, and an increasingly demonstrative sharing of affection. Amanda was changing.

In her two remaining years at HML, she regularly passed by my classroom for a hug, and time permitting, a chat. She was growing in front of my eyes, both literally and figuratively, and as she neared the end of her senior year, had become a young woman. She had served as an officer in the National Honor Society, and was excited about my attending the upcoming National Honor Society Breakfast a few weeks later. At that inspirational event, when after breakfast the time had come for the NHS officers to present the Teacher Superlative awards to their respective recipients, Amanda stood at the microphone and spoke lovingly and proudly of the time she had spent with me, and of the qualities that she and the other NHS members felt made me the logical choice as (male) "Most Dedicated Teacher" at HML. Her remarks had been prefaced with her announcement that I would be retiring from HML, and the one-two punch of that fact, in conjunction with the award I was to receive after just a few more steps to the dais, brought a heartfelt eruption from the students and adults in attendance at the breakfast. Amanda met me before I reached her spot at the microphone, and we hugged for quite a few moments, before I turned, humbly waved to the crowd, and returned to my seat. I saw Amanda one last time at graduation, and then she was off; off to college and her successful future-in-waiting.

Mr.Ringler,

I'm so happy I got to have you twice in my high school career. I still remember sitting in your class as a freshman, terrified of the rest of the school, but always feeling safe in your classroom. I cannot imagine how HML's future students will cope without you as their teacher, because your wisdom, wittiness, and lovable nature will be missed. I wish you would stay at HML for many years to come, so that every student that walks these halls will have the chance to say that they have been inspired by your greatness. Since it's not possible, I will do my best to tell everyone just how amazing you are.

Good luck with all that you do once you retire, though I doubt you'll need it. You are so amazing and so great an individual that no one will ever be able to take your place.

Have a great summer, and I hope we'll stay in touch.

P.S. You have always been my favorite teacher at HML !

Your student,

Amanda

"Hey Ricardo, you can't sleep in class. Get up, pal." More often than not, that was how I brought Ricardo back from his all too frequent naps during the first year he was with me in English I Honors. If he wasn't participating in a discussion or reading aloud to the class, he was drifting away, with his neck bending and his head lowering ever nearer to his desk. Ricardo was a bright student, with so much potential, but he was sleeping it all away. Time has a way of slipping by all too quickly, and I could see it slipping away from Ricardo, as his ninth grade experience was fading right in front of his droopy eyes. I'm a pretty forceful and animated speaker, and a kid would have to be really tired to fall asleep with my voice as his or her lullaby, but Ricardo seemed to be more than capable of doing that. There was no physical ailment according to his family, he just may have been staying up too late at night, as was the case with many other teenagers. Somehow, through constant prodding and nudging, and having enlisted the aid of his classroom neighbors, each of whom I had duly deputized as "Ricardo waker-uppers", we managed to get him through the year, albeit with a less than exemplary final grade.

I've mentioned that a number of my students moved along with me from ninth to tenth grade when I began teaching English II, both Honors and Regular. Ricardo was among that unique group, once again to be my student for another year of English. He had matured a bit, and his sleeping episodes became less frequent, though they still occasionally made an appearance. The more awake he was, the more effective he was as a student, and the year went more smoothly than the one before. I found myself really beginning to get to know the real Ricardo, the intelligent, curious, warped sense of humor Ricardo. We talked a great deal about a multitude of topics, from sports to music to movies to college plans, and I felt confident that things were looking up for this polite and respectful boy.

Passing by my room on a regular basis throughout his junior and senior years, I no longer recognized Ricardo. He was a head taller than before, and presented an air of maturity and confidence that apparently had been just waiting for the right moment to bloom. I'd seen that remarkable transformation in other kids over the years. When people would ask me what I believed to be the difference between ninth graders and tenth graders, I usually said "Five years!" Freshman come in as middle school babies and, after having their eyes opened in that first year of high school, many of them mature quickly, leaving their middle school mentality behind. That phenomenon often, though not in all cases, continues to occur in the upper grades as well, producing juniors, and ultimately, seniors, who are light years ahead of the little kids they had been when they first entered high school. Something about the imminent arrival of the outside world freezes them in their tracks; frightened deer in the headlights of a speeding car on a dark, misty night. Well, Ricardo was in the process of making that transformation, and I felt far more secure that he was well on his way. At my frequent Coffee House performances, Ricardo, a member of the Chorus family, was always there to assist Eric Firestone with the setting up of the Chorus Room. He never missed an opportunity to let me know just how proud of me he was, that he loved my music and my live performances. That meant more than you might think to an old guy like me, knowing that a teenager had actually been touched by the words I had written, and the chords I had played, and the voice with which I had sung.

The true measure of Ricardo's burgeoning maturity came with a short time left to go in his senior year. I hadn't seen him in the hall in a while, but while en route to the Main Office during a planning period, I saw him walking with his father, heading towards the main entrance of the school. "Hey Ricardo!" I said as I made my way in their direction. Something wasn't right, I felt it. After saying hello to his father, a wonderful man whom I had never met, though I had often heard about, I asked if everything was okay. Ricardo looked up at his father and softly asked if it was okay for him to tell me. "Come on, he's Mr. Ringler. Tell him." Ricardo's mother had passed away within the past week. Heart problems had gotten the best of her, and she was gone. What can you do in a situation like that? I grabbed Ricardo and held him to me as I would my own son or daughter in a time of crisis. I fought back tears as best I could, but the pain I felt for this wonderful kid and his father, and the vivid memory of my own father's passing just a year before, overwhelmed me for a moment, and my eyes welled despite my best efforts. I hugged his father too, imagining the emptiness by which he too must have felt surrounded. I told Ricardo to stop by my room any time, morning or afternoon, whenever he needed to talk, or just needed a hug and a shoulder to lean on. "You go to him." his father said. "It's Mr. Ringler, so you go to him. Sit with him and talk." They thanked me one final time for my support, and turned to go to the parking lot. I decided against continuing to the Main Office, choosing instead to return to my room, my sanctuary at the moment, a place where I could gather myself, and think about the years I had known Ricardo, wondering how he would do with this sudden and heart wrenching loss.

The final few days of school found me with a small video camera in my hands, one that I had brought from home in order to capture the thoughts of my students as they prepared to watch me ride off into the sunset. Kids were stopping by from everywhere to say goodbye, and of course, Ricardo made his way to my classroom, signing my yearbook as I signed his. When I asked him if he wanted to say a few words for the camera, he delivered an impromptu dedication to me, thanking me for tolerating him during his early years, and for remaining his friend since then. His words of gratitude for my having been there after the loss of his mother were almost too touching to bear, and his "I love you Ringler", among the most beautiful gifts I had ever received. I love you too Ricardo, and I'll talk to you soon.

Dear Ringler,

I've had the amazing pleasure of being your student for my freshman and sophomore years. 2 years down the line and you've become a father figure and a great friend. From sleeping in your class to clapping for a performance of yours at the many Coffee Houses, it's been a blast. HML is losing one of its best. With your witty humor and hilarious remarks, you've made HML an amazing and pleasurable place to be. Over the past few weeks I should also be grateful to have you in my life, for getting me through the toughest part. This loss has been great, but your words of comfort are something I keep in mind to get me through this. I love you Ringler. I wish you the best of luck in the future and in your musician career as well.

Much love, from your best and favorite student,

Ricardo

For six years I had kept myself at bay, assuming an unofficial leadership role within the school while serving as a teacher. For the past few years, my friend Michael Garcia, who would ultimately serve for four years as Language Arts Department Chair, had indicated to me that he had had enough of the position, and wanted to step away from it. As I explained in a much earlier chapter of the book, Michael was, and remains, an amazing English teacher. At HML however, a state designated "low performing" school, he clearly wanted no part of the FCAT scene. He asked me if I would be interested in once again becoming department chair, and after spending a few days thinking it through, I said I would be willing to do so. To make a long story short, which for me is not always easy to do, Michael stepped aside at year's end, and I was appointed Language Arts Department Chair for the 2009-2010 school year by our latest principal, Christopher Shinn, who was about to begin his second year at HML.

Chapter 21

One late summer afternoon in July 2008, while I was in the computer lab classroom in which I taught night school, (I haven't mentioned night school yet, have I? I taught for a total of fourteen years in that program, originally to pay for the college educations of both my son and my wife who attended college at the same time as I didn't qualify for financial aid because I made too much money as a teacher, and thereafter because it gave me the opportunity to save a few dollars. Yes, I know – in the eyes of the public, teachers make far too much money, work far too few hours, and virtually bankrupt their respective state's budgets and overall financial stability. Sorry Mr. And Mrs. John Q., but you're wrong.) I happened to glance into the hallway near the Main Office, where I saw an extremely tall man walking with the school's zone mechanic, my friend Bruce. Having no idea who this stranger was, I stepped out to say hello to Bruce, and was immediately introduced to Mr. Christopher Shinn, our new principal.

Mr. Shinn, hereafter referred to as Chris, had come to HML from Barbara Goleman Senior High School, one of our rival schools located just a few miles away. He had been serving there as an assistant principal, and had now been given the opportunity and responsibility to bring HML back to its glory days. I welcomed him to our school, wished him good luck, and stated that if there was any way in which I could be of service, he simply had to ask. He thanked me and moved on to resume his inspection of the school.

One thing that struck the faculty during Chris's first year was how genuinely interested he was in his students and his staff.

He was an approachable and generous soul, and before the year was out, I actually felt a little hint of the old HML family spirit beginning to reappear and thrive. HML was always like a family. Many schools have similar environments, but one of the qualities that immediately struck our many visitors was the overall feeling that people at HML liked being there, enjoyed working with each other, and longed to recapture the powerful traditions of HML's storied past. Chris conveyed that very same attitude in everything he tried to do while at our school. The students loved him, as did the overwhelming majority of the faculty and staff. He cared about people, and as a result, they wanted to do well for him. His style was not management by intimidation, but true leadership by showing people that they mattered and could make a difference. He knew he had much to learn about being a high school principal, and was unafraid to ask for guidance and help any time he felt it necessary. Hialeah-Miami Lakes Senior High School was, however, a rare and unique animal. No matter what Chris tried to do, and despite his, and our, best efforts, our FCAT results at the end of his first year were lower than expected, and failed to elevate our state report card grade from the previous year. Thus, we were once again a "D" school, with much work left to do.

The intention of this book is not to denigrate or demean, and by no stretch of the imagination is it a "tell-all" book. I have tried faithfully to extoll the virtues of the school I loved for nearly twenty-nine years, and to share my memories of some of the students and adults I came to know and love during my HML career. I have always understood the pressures faced by the good folks in charge of Miami-Dade County Public Schools, and by their counterparts at the regional and school levels. I want to believe that when the district sent a virtual army of support staff to our school during Chris's second year, it was in an effort to bolster the efforts of the hard-working faculty and staff, and to hopefully provide assistance in preparation for that year's FCAT onslaught. There were district people, however, some of whom had actually been assigned to HML for an extended period of time, looking over Chris's shoulder from morning until afternoon. Providing support is one thing, making someone feel like he or she can't handle his or her own position without constant "guidance" is another. As I had once again become Language Arts Department Chair that year, I was privy to many of the "goings on" that were taking place, and I could clearly see the effect the pressure was having on Chris. Yes, I know. He was a principal and was being paid to handle such stress. To me, however, this seemed to be going far beyond that, and he deserved better.

That year, his second at HML, Chris became seriously ill, requiring surgery and a an extended period of recovery before returning to HML at the beginning of May 2010, a day or so before our scheduled SACS Evaluation Team visit was to begin. (Incredibly, five years had already passed since our previous SACS experience.) In his absence, the entire school had pulled together under the auspices of our leadership team of assistant principals and department chairs, firmly keeping the goal of FCAT success in sight, wanting desperately to make Chris proud, and to get the school report card grade "monkey" off his back. In my additional role as SACS Chair, I had once again been called upon over the past year and a half to lead the school towards a successful continuation of our accreditation, and rather than belabor the point, suffice it to say that we were indeed rewarded for our efforts with another five-years as a fully accredited institution. Chris's arrival at school just prior to the SACS visit seemed to spark everyone back to life, and an endless parade of well-wishers stopped by to see him and to welcome him home.

When the year ended, and students and staff had left for the summer, I was told that Chris was being assigned to another school – a small "law enforcement academy" magnet high school in downtown Miami. The next day after receiving that news, I drove down to school to teach my night school class (night school ran on a different schedule than day school, so it would still be in session until July.), and stopped by Chris's office to say goodbye as he would be leaving within a day or two. I was angry, but he seemed to be at peace with the decision, happy about his new opportunity. If he was okay, I told him, then I was okay. Inside, I was not okay. I am a firm believer that when you hire a principal to implement change, you have to allow time, at least four or five years, for those changes to be implemented, and for their subsequent effects to be realized. I felt so strongly that HML was finally back on track, at least to some degree, and the state's school grade for Chris's final year, the one we received after he had left HML, indicated that perhaps his stay with us should have lasted a while longer. For the first time in quite a few years, we had earned a "C" grade; maybe not exemplary, but for a school digging its way back up, a hell of a start.

I was in touch with Chris a few times after his departure for the Law Enforcement Academy. He seemed quite pleased with the success of his new school, and later asked me if I wanted to join his faculty for the next year as an English teacher. Remember that part of the book where I explained how my daily round trip to HML was seventy miles a day? Well, Chris's new school was located in the heart of downtown Miami, and that would have increased my round trip to over one hundred miles a day. Factor in the increased drive time and the extra expense for gas, and you get the picture. It just would not have been feasible for me to transfer to a school even further away from home, so I had to contact Chris and turn down his generous offer. I would have loved to work with him again, but some things are just not in the cards. I always have, and always will, wish nothing but wonderful things for Chris, and he is one of the people I miss the most.

Chapter 22

An English II Honors Gifted class. In 2009-2010, for the first time in my career, I was scheduled to teach a gifted class. It was to be small group of sixteen students, all of whom had been in the Gifted Program for a number of years, and had taken English I Honors Gifted the previous year with my friend Michael Garcia. These were the kids who participated in clubs, played in the school band or on athletic teams, and represented HML at various academic competitions. They were bright and inquisitive, frequently approaching their classes from a slightly different angle, but for the most part, were responsible and well-prepared. Upon meeting the class for the first time, I could immediately see the direction I was going to have to take with these students. I'm a "discusser". I loved discussing literature, goals, and life in general with my kids, and with this group of sixteen, I felt that I would be able to take those discussions to an even higher level. I was right! An endless stream of perceptive questions frequently followed the reading of a piece of literature, oftentimes segueing into open ended discussions about related, or unrelated, topics. I found myself truly enjoying the academic and intellectual stimulation of the class.

Many of these wonderful kids would ultimately rise as juniors and seniors to become the future leaders of the school, assuming leadership roles in Yearbook, National Honor Society, Model U.N., and a host of other academic pursuits. They would be accepted to a variety of colleges and universities, receiving numerous scholarships. All of them were capable of success, but while with me as tenth graders, not all of them found the right road to take them there.

I loved Karen, our future top senior, and Elizabeth, sweetness and light personified. Ashlie was an athlete, along with being a top notch student, and Kassandra quietly moved along, amassing success after success in her classes, but almost without being noticed due to her reserved demeanor. Kimberly, a bit more exuberant perhaps than some of the others, was always "heard" in one way or another. She had exceedingly strong opinions about a variety of subjects, and rarely kept them to herself. But, she was a great student and a powerful force. There were two Chriss-es in the class; one a baseball player, and the other a tall, imposingly large, boy of great depth and curiosity. Overall, this was a great collection of students.

There was also Edan; I haven't mentioned Edan yet, have I? Edan was a boy of tremendous potential, one surely destined for success, both in school and thereafter in his chosen career. Like me, he was a devout Beatles fan, and was very much into music in general. As the year progressed, and he heard about my little side career as a recording artist, he ordered a few of my albums, providing us with even more to discuss. I loved Edan, but I was quite concerned about his lack of effort in class, and how he seemed at times to distance himself from his studies and his potential. We talked about this regularly, and he produced with flashes of what he could be, but he still lagged behind. Later, as a senior, Edan loved to recall the time when he had politely, but firmly, refused to do an assignment in my class, and was more than willing to accept the inevitable "F" he thought he would receive as a consequence. My reaction to his refusal seemed to shock him a bit. "Sorry, but I won't accept that from you. I won't let you decide to not do the work. You'll just have to complete the assignment. You're an Honors Gifted student, and not completing your assignment is not acceptable to me, and should not be to you either." Edan spent a few minutes by himself at his desk, revisiting internally the conflict he had created, and my response to his stand. He said nothing more about the assignment, and quietly left the classroom when the bell rang a short while later. At the beginning of our next class together, he submitted the completed assignment to me, I thanked him and told him how much I respected this quantum leap in maturity, and we never talked about it again, at least not until the following year, when as a junior he had begun to blossom into the student he was capable of being. He thanked me for refusing to allow him to fail, and for my patience and generosity in allowing him to submit his assignment, late though it was, without penalty. I responded by saying that the assignment itself had nothing to do with it. It was the need to complete "everything", and to fulfill his responsibilities that was in question. I frequently referred to the "outside world" in my delivering of life lessons to my students. My corporate background gave me that right, and my kids needed to know that as much as they thought they were indeed the center of the universe, they weren't, and no future boss of theirs was going to accept a refusal to complete work by providing additional time for the work to be submitted. They would be shown the door and replaced by someone else who was more conscientious. Some of them understood immediately, and some of them would come to understand in time. Life is great teacher, better than the best teacher you've ever had. Edan understood, and he never looked back. By his senior year, he had moved to the forefront of the school, an academic success and a leader in every way, even having been appointed as president of the National Honor Society. He had matured by light years, and whenever he passed by to say hello, he'd hug me in that "guy" way of hugging, knowing that his days at HML were numbered. His yearbook inscription to me found

Edan confident, and eager to tackle his university career. With a greeting to me which began with "Ringler (though I suppose I'll be calling you "Mike" now)", it was clear to me that this heretofore underachiever had risen to the top of his game, and was truly ready for the challenges waiting for him at the university level.

Ringler (though I suppose I'll be calling you "Mike" now),

You're already aware that HML won't be the same place without you and that your past students can't imagine it; this is because as you've been made fully aware of over the years, you are one of the kindest, most generous, wisest people to have ever stepped foot in these halls. You are one of the few people who I can honestly say I cannot describe – words fail me when I try to say just how great and influential you are, not just as a man or a teacher, but also as a friend, musician, and just about anything else you set yourself to being. This is why students are happy despite your departure. We know that wherever he is, Ringler will be the best at what he does. Even though I know you won't need it, I'm wishing you luck as you leave HML, wherever that takes you. I won't let this be the last you hear from me either.

To my inspiration with love,

Edan

Chapter 23

July 2010 brought yet another new principal to Hialeah-Miami Lakes Senior High School, Jose Bueno. Jose had previously served as principal of Country Club Middle School for the past few years, and had guided the school to two successive state report card "A" grades, no easy task. My first time meeting Jose was on a summer day when he was being escorted around the campus by the departing Chris Shinn. Now that was a sight to see; the at least six foot five Chris walking side by side with the much shorter Jose, probably five foot seven or so. Hey, I'm five foot eleven, and I felt like a baby brother standing next to Chris! Chris called me over to meet Jose, and I found him to be a pleasant young man. Suddenly, I was older than EVERYBODY, and every adult had become either a young man or young woman to me. When the hell had that happened? I had been older than Chris by twelve years or so, and now found myself older than my new principal by probably sixteen years! This was getting ridiculous, and I would have no more of it, deciding that I had had enough of getting older, and thus would thereafter stop my procession of birthdays, choosing instead to remain at age fifty-nine for the rest of my days. But, I digress!

Jose was possessed of a strong personality, and a record of success that obviously the district hoped would translate well at HML in its quest to return as a premier high school. As the final pages of that summer were turned, and the next chapter of the book of HML was waiting to be written, the start of the new school year found the entire HML family ready, willing, and able to support our new principal. Jose brought with him a well-defined set of objectives and goals, but they were based upon factors relevant to his previous school. HML is a different animal, it always has been. It is a school faced with a variety of problem areas covering a variety of student demographic groupings. Large numbers of students from low income families, non-English speaking families, and no families at all, walk side by side with the remainder of the school's population every day. Most high schools have to deal with one of these factors, maybe two at most, but almost none of them have to deal with all three, plus others that I have not even included. Yes, HML is a different animal.

Jose is a bright man, highly skilled, and with the vision to recognize the needs of a school. By the end of his first year at HML, however, we had missed the mark. Jose had admittedly somewhat miscalculated the solutions to HML's needs, and we fell short of maintaining the "C" grade which we had earned during Chris Shinn's final year, being awarded a "D" instead. It was so painful to hear that damned "D" grade again. We had just risen up from the ashes a year before, and this all too familiar territory was a morale buster for everyone at HML. Instead of retreating, Jose instead chose a different path. Using an end of year principal evaluation survey that he had created, and which he had asked every faculty member to complete, Jose looked inward and truly considered the areas in which he was deemed in need of improvement, working hard at improving those areas before the next year had begun. On a number of occasions I told him how proud I was of him, older guy to younger guy, for accepting the feedback of the faculty, recognizing his shortcomings (no pun intended), and then actively working to improve in those areas. Not many leaders will be man, or woman, enough to go that route, but Jose was, and I believe he came out on the other side a better principal for it. This new and improved Jose then set out to delve into the very fabric that was HML.

2010-2011 introduced a new event to HML, a "Coffee House" fund-raiser to be sponsored by Eric Firestone, the industrious and multi-talented Chorus Director and vocal teacher who had been at HML for the past few years. Under his tutelage, HML's various choral groups had won numerous awards at district and state levels, and had also been called upon to perform at a variety of district functions. Eric approached me one day, probably in February or March, to ask if I would be willing to perform a few songs at the first Coffee House. The concept of this new fund raiser would be simple: students from Eric's advanced Chorus classes would perform in the Chorus Room, in front of an audience comprised of anyone who cared to show up and pay the $5.00 admission fee, which would then entitle them to all of the coffee or hot chocolate they cared to drink. Having been a fan of my music, and having purchased a number of my albums to date, Eric thought the kids would love to hear a few of my tracks performed live. I immediately said I would perform, but as I was still teaching night school on Mondays and Wednesdays at that time, I would need the show to be scheduled for a Tuesday or Thursday. Thursday it would be, and I began rehearsing for my mini-gig almost immediately. One thing I didn't want to do was screw anything up, especially as I would be playing some of my songs, as well as a Beatles tune or two. On the day of the first of many Coffee Houses, I had brought all of the equipment I would need in order to give the audience the fullest possible renditions of a few of the songs that appeared on my albums. Setting everything up on the tiny Chorus Room stage after school had ended took a while, and my subsequent sound checks took a while longer, but in short order I was ready to go. A few finishing touches on the decorations that filled the room, and a last minute check by Eric and his helpers of the coffee, hot chocolate, and baked goods, and the students and adults who had been patiently waiting outside were finally allowed into the makeshift concert hall. There were spotlights on the stage, and balloons and banners covering nearly every inch of the walls. Indeed, a grand event was about to unfold. I was introduced as the first act, and I immediately launched into a couple of songs from my 2009 album "We Have Liftoff", songs that had received limited airplay on small radio stations in Australia, Canada, England, and yes, even the United States. The excitement from those in attendance was palpable, and I loved every ounce of it. I had played in front of many audiences over the years, sometimes in my role as a drummer and singer in the bands I've already mentioned in this book, and since 2007, as a solo artist occasionally performing at a few local venues, accompanied by my "band" of my own prerecorded backing tracks to provide as rich a sound as possible when my live guitar and vocals were added into the mix. Though I had enjoyed many gigs in the past, either as a drummer and singer, or as a solo artist with a guitar slung over his shoulder, I'd never had as much fun as I had playing for the large group of kids and adults who attended that first Coffee House. There were many more Coffee Houses to follow that year and the next, all the way up until the last one of the year in April 2012, just a couple of months before I retired. I had literally just told my administration that late April 26 morning of my upcoming retirement, and though I had informed my departments immediately afterwards, I had not yet shared the decision with any of my students. That painful task would begin the next morning. Therefore, I had kept the secret to myself, and the "band" played on at that final Coffee House. Once I had indeed shared my plan with my students and a number of my non-departmental colleagues, I specifically went to see Eric Firestone to tell him the news. After his initial shock, I stated my intentions of returning to perform at future Coffee House if at all possible, an idea he was so excited to hear. A few days later, after he had shared my news with his students, as well as my plan to continue performing, he passed along to me the deep appreciation of his students, who were thrilled to know that I would not turn my back on them. I had been involved with the school's music programs in one way or another for almost my entire teaching career, and the fact that I was no longer going to be employed at the school did not mean that I would stop supporting those programs. The new school year has just started, and I await Eric's call to me, announcing the date of the first Coffee House of the year. Many of my students will be there, and it will feel like I never left.

Chapter 24

Within my first years as a teacher, I learned that virtually every kid has a "story": perhaps a life of many blessings and good fortune; perhaps one of hardship and loss and pain; or most often, an amalgam of elements, much like most of us. Every day of my career, no matter which classroom(s) I had been assigned to, I stood at my door in the hallway, and greeted every student as they entered, not to mention every student who simply passed by, my student or not. (I suppose that seemed odd to a few of our less than sociable kids, but you can't say I didn't try.) My goal was to have every single student feel worthwhile and cared about, no matter what else might have been going on in their lives at that moment. "Who is this crazy man?" some of them must have thought as they entered my room, especially on the first or second day of school. In my heart though, I knew that if I was always there for them, if I showed them every time I saw them how important they were to me, then they would feel that my classroom was a place worth coming to, a protective harbor in which they could moor themselves and feel safe. In time, as I grew to know my kids, I could see their lives reflected in their eyes as they entered the room. There were the brightly shining eyes of the kids who had just met with some particular success in school, or who had just celebrated a birthday, and there were the downward cast, red-rimmed eyes of the child who had just lost a loved one, or who had just been told that his or her parents were separating, or who was simply overwhelmed by the pressures of being a teenager. Those were the ones I pulled to one side, asking them if they were okay, and reminding them that I was there if they needed to talk. I told them that in addition to being a teacher, I was also a father, and eventually, a grandfather, and that I understood. While some of them were initially hesitant to divulge much, if any, information, many responded almost immediately, either by standing in the hallway with me after class had started, or by asking if they could sit and talk with me during lunch. Most of stories I heard over the years were the "usual" trials and tribulations of the average teenager. Sometimes, however, more often than I would have expected, I was made privy to numerous situations of a more serious nature, frequently leaving me unable to do anything but hold a child in my arms and let them release the tears that may have lain silently dormant for far too long. Of course, there were also those instances that required the intervention of a counselor, or administrator, or on rare occasion, a telephone call to an appropriate state government agency. Yes, I had students who were being abused, both physically and emotionally, by parents or guardians, and yes, though thankfully not in recent times, I had kids who were involved with drugs. I had far too many kids who had lost a parent, or sibling, and who had not been able to cope with such powerful loss. What the hell can you tell a child whose father, mother, sister, or brother has just passed away? There are no words that can assuage the hurt in a child's heart and make it all better. I would have given anything at those times to make it all better, but there was nothing I could offer other than supportive words, a shoulder upon which to cry, and arms within which to be enveloped and protected. I had kids who were being bullied or taunted by other kids. In some cases I handled those situations in my own way, and sometimes I handled them by escorting my student to an administrator. These kids were my kids, my family, and they were not going to go through the "bad stuff" alone. I had sworn that to myself when I first walked through the doors of HML, and hopefully, I never let a kid feel alone.

Keonni was a bright light in my English II Honors program in 2010-2011. My goodness, she was perceptive, sharp as a tack, and a wonderfully expressive reader. I watched her in awe at times, wondering just how far this kid could go. Then she began to miss class, first once in a while, then for days or even a few weeks on end. A telephone call to her mother provided me with an answer, though not one which I wanted to hear. Keonni was suffering from Crohn's Disease, a painful and debilitating condition with which she had been dealing for years. Medications and diet had enabled her to live a fairly normal life, but there were always going to be periods of time in which the Crohn's got the better of her, leaving her either hospitalized or homebound. Her absences were a direct result of this, and her mother was seriously concerned about her missing so much class time and falling behind with her written work. I sent work home for her, but also told her mother that if Keonni was unable to complete it, she could simply make it up when she returned to school. Her health was of paramount importance to me, and I had no qualms about her ability to catch up with everything, which she did in full upon her return. She was out a few more days here and there throughout the year, but she finally made it through to the end. As a junior the next year, she stopped by frequently to see me, and appeared in better overall health than when she was with me, though there was one span of a few weeks where she had spent time in the hospital. For the remainder of that year, she seemed to be in school mostly every day, stopping by for a hug and a smile. Now that I've gone, I'll have to wait until her graduation for a hug, and to see that smile once again.

Chapter 25

For so long, one of my best friends and most loyal supporters was HML's Media Specialist, Gloria Flores, a woman who had been with Miami-Dade County Public Schools far longer than I. Over the years, we had had many conversations about so many of the goings on at HML, frequently, though not always, seeing eye to eye. We discussed district and state initiatives, administrative decisions, programs, staffing, health issues, a million things. Gloria was an extremely outspoken woman, and though she would approach the sharing of her opinions in a most professional and dignified manner at all times, there was never any doubt about where she stood on any number of issues. She was in charge of one of the finest high school library/media centers in the system, and was constantly looking for ways by which to upgrade and improve services for HML's students, many of whom spent long hours there before and after school, doing homework, writing reports, and yes, even READING! HML's students knew they could depend upon her, and that she was there to assist them in any way possible.

A few years back, Gloria came to me to share some bad news. She had just been diagnosed with breast cancer, and as Karen Stemer would do a few years later, was going on medical leave to fight the good fight. Her attitude was nothing but positive, her goal nothing short of returning to HML upon completion of her treatment. After a yearlong battle, Gloria returned to school, to the Media Center, exactly where she belonged. She remained one of my closest friends, and was one of the very first people to whom I revealed my retirement plans. She was on the same page with me in that area, and she often sought me out, looking for my input about various insurance offerings and pension options, knowing that I had studied such matters closely. When I first presented her the idea of my retiring that June, she was incredibly supportive of my decision, happy that I would be getting out while I was still young enough (Yes, young enough! I would be fifty-nine, not ninety-nine, for God's sake!) to do some other things that I had in mind. We spoke often during the last few months of my final year, knowing that those conversations would likely be among the last of the frequent ones we would have. We will speak again on the occasions when I return to HML for one reason or another, and will surely communicate by telephone or email, but one way or another, we will stay in touch.

Arriving at 6:20am every day had its advantages: a few moments to chat with the four or five other early birds, or to vent about a few things here and there; just a bit of breathing space to get ready for the upcoming school day and the madness it might bring. I'd always needed that extra buffer zone of time in the morning, knowing that my "to do list" was brimming with a multitude of tasks just waiting for me to check them off one by one.

Though I enjoyed the company of most of my morning compatriots, the one with whom I connected most closely was Carolyn Spina, the principal's secretary for many years. She had served in that role throughout the terms of four principals, and had truly been my "go to" person for that entire span. There was nobody else on whom I could depend for a straighter answer, or with whom I could have a more heartfelt discussion, than Carolyn. We talked about school, family, religion, life, and just about any other topic that called out for our input, and whether or not we always agreed on every aspect of every topic, we always respected each other's points of view and ended our discussions as friends. Her children had been HML students years before, and she had served in other roles within the school prior to being reassigned as the principal's secretary, so she had a powerful, long term bond with the school and its glorious history. A woman of unfailing integrity, one of her qualities that I most admired, Carolyn pulled no punches, whether speaking with the principal or any other employee. If someone were approaching her desk and saw "that face", they knew better than to continue in that direction, and would abruptly stop and reverse direction, returning when the atmosphere had cleared a bit. Yet, there was nobody nicer and more generous than Carolyn. She was the first one to volunteer to help anybody at any time, handling whatever needed handling in a most professional and cooperative manner. Professional – that's the exact word for Carolyn.

After having served for so many years, and knowing that principal Chris Shinn was leaving for another school, Carolyn made the difficult decision to retire from HML at the end of the 2009-2010 school year. Word spread quickly throughout the school, and I wondered who was going to help me with everything with which she had always helped me, and who was I going to act silly with and bother in the early morning fluorescent light of the main office. Oh, I could get very silly in my unofficial role as morning talk show host, and Carolyn's response was always the same; "Michael, stop that!", inserted in between her bouts of laughter. Maybe that's what I miss most about Carolyn, she understood me, knew the person I was and where my heart lay. Since leaving, we've been in touch a few times by email, or via her visits to HML for one reason or another. I made sure while I was still at HML that if someone let on that Carolyn was "in the house", often times with her husband Mike Uspensky, HML's former football coach and counselor, I found her, to say hello and to let her know how things were going. She never forgets to send my family a Chanukah card every year, and she never forgets the silly English teacher and department chair who always tried his best to make her mornings a little brighter.

Chapter 26

My eighth period English II Honors class in 2010-2011 brought two wonderful blessings into my life; Angeli and Sasha. In a class filled with a number of good kids, many of whom were also strong students, these two little dynamos filled my days with warmth and laughter. As they later told me, they were at first quite intimidated by my strong personality, thinking that I was probably going to be the strictest teacher they had ever encountered. In time, as they found their fears unwarranted, and had discovered just how good an actor I had been, they warmed to me, and we have been close ever since. Both of them continued to visit me regularly after moving on to eleventh grade, the year that I made the decision to retire. They, along with so many other students, made me swear an oath that I would be at their graduation a year later, and of course, I will.

I love Sasha. She's such a hard-working and honest girl, with her goals clearly in focus all of the time. During our numerous discussions, both when she was with me as a sophomore, and when she would return as a junior to my room for a chat, she displayed a maturity and level of common sense that belied her years, always leaving me confident that she was not only going to succeed, but would succeed on her terms. Forthright and fiery, there was never any doubt where Sasha stood on a variety of issues, and she cared little about what others might or might not have thought of her when she expressed her opinions. As a member of the HML's outstanding HOSA (Health Occupation Students of America) program, Sasha was establishing herself as not only a dedicated student, but as a true leader who was respected by all, as demonstrated by her selection as president of that organization for her upcoming senior year.

There had been a few occasions during my final two years at HML where the tables had turned, and I was the one facing some serious issues. One thing I had always tried to do as a teacher was leave my problems outside of my classroom and go about my business as best as I could. I had done that in 1984 when my mother had passed away on one of the two teacher work days just prior to the start of the 1984-1985 school year, and in late April 2011 I had to once again travel that road when my father passed away at age 95. The telephone rang that morning at 4:15, and I knew he was gone. While the wonderful hospice folks and the nursing care facility would be taking care of a few things, there were many others that would need my immediate attention that day, and in the days to follow. I quickly called the "substitute" telephone number at school to arrange for class coverage, something I had only done nine times before in my nearly twenty-nine year teaching career, told my wife that I was going to head down to school to prepare plans and materials for the next three days, and would then return home to start making the necessary arrangements. Everything went well over the next few days, thank you very much, with my father having been given a full military burial in honor of his having not only served in the army during World War II, but also for the wounds he had received in battle and the six months he had spent as a prisoner of war in a German prison camp. Upon my return to school, a half hour before classes were to begin, Sasha came bursting into my classroom, wrapped her arms around me, and told me everything was going to be okay. She said that was there for me, just as I had always been for her, and my other students. We talked for a while, and the maturity and wisdom in her eyes and in her voice were astounding. Here was this little peanut comforting me, as would many other students throughout that day and in the days that followed, but she was a part of that special group, the ones who were most like family to me, and her soothing words of comfort and her desire to protect me touched me so deeply that the video of that morning will be playing inside my mind for quite some time. Sasha and I have spoken a few times by telephone, with a few emails thrown in for good measure, during my first summer as a retired person, and we will most assuredly be in touch throughout the year. What I will miss the most though, will be standing at my classroom door, seeing the distant image of a usually curly headed little girl walking steadily towards me from far down the hall, coming closer and closer until she is standing right in front of me, ready with a warm embrace, a quick "Love you Ringler!", and a "See you later.", as she hurries on to her next class.

Dear RIngler,

Sophomore year was amazing with you. You truly have made a big impact on my life. Sometimes, I sit and wonder what I'll do without you next year. I mean, you have been there for absolutely everything! I love you with all my heart and I hope you don't EVER forget that I'm always your #1.

Love always,

Sasha

Dear Ringler,

I already signed your yearbook, but there wasn't enough room to say everything I wanted. Words aren't enough to share all of the memories we've shared. I can see how much it hurts for you to say goodbye, but I am proud of you for staying strong. Just remember that goodbye now doesn't mean I won't see you again; I will. Just keep your head up Ringler. You made a choice that was right for YOU and I respect you for that. All I want is for you to be happy Ringler. You have had such a big impact on my life, it's scary. You've been there for me from the first moment. One day you told me something and it's something I want you to remember: No matter what happens today, the sun will shine tomorrow and it will be a new day." I love you mister.

Love,

Sasha

On the day before Father's Day 2012, a split second before its fourth ring would awaken the soundly sleeping answering machine, I answered the telephone. A tiny voice exclaimed "Hi Mr. Ringler, it's Angeli." A week and a half had passed since I had walked away from HML for the last time, at least as an employee. That initial stage of my transition into retirement from Miami-Dade County Public Schools had been difficult for me. Literally half of my life had been spent at that school, and as you now know, there were half a lifetime's memories inside my heart and my head, lovingly stored for a later time, perhaps to be recalled for inclusion in a book such as this one. No question, I was going to miss being at HML for a number of reasons, though I knew I had made the correct decision by retiring at the time I did. While there were many of my colleagues whom I would miss, it was the kids whom I would miss the most. I missed them already. And then, I heard that tiny voice, and the love and affection deep within it, and I excitedly proclaimed "Angeli !". After a brief review of the oh so many things that had transpired for each of us in the past nine days, Angeli inquired as to what I was doing on Father's Day. I explained that our son was most likely going to be with us for the early part of that day due to some afternoon business responsibilities he had to attend to, but that we had no other plans after that. "Can I come and see you? I'd like to spend part of Father's Day with you." The rewards of such an exchange are incalculable, they simply cannot be measured. After quickly presenting Angeli's request to my wife, just to confirm that she was comfortable with the idea, which she was, I told Angeli that we would love to have her spend time with us, and that I was honored that she wished to spend part of that special day with me. Sadly, her parents had divorced when she was a little girl, and her father, who eventually remarried and had additional children with his second wife, apparently did not connect well with Angeli, leaving the relationship between the two of them in a fractured and deteriorating state over the years. She loved her father, and still does, but she found herself on the outside of his life.

Angeli's time with us was a delight. My wife Rella and she were simpatico right from the start, a natural progression as they had spoken a few times on the telephone when my wife had called during class, or while I was in the middle of a planning period during which Angeli had sauntered into my room from her class next door, with her teacher's permission of course. Their first conversation was the result of my wife asking me how to load photos onto her Facebook page, and as Angeli was quite adept at things like that, I passed the call over to her. The two of them talked for a bit before the step by step instructions were delivered, and then the two of them said goodbye. When she had stepped out of her car in front of our condominium, she had a beautiful, glittering gift bag in her hands, a Father's Day package for me. When I said that she shouldn't have spent her money that way, she replied "But it's Father's Day!" For the next four hours, the exuberance and depth of this wonderfully bright girl were on full display, often leaving my wife and me laughing, and at times, completely mesmerized. She sat next to me on the couch, shoulder to shoulder, and entertained us with story after story about school, and her water polo and soccer team adventures. When the sun was beginning its early evening retreat, I told Angeli that I didn't want her to drive home in the dark, so I suggested that she leave, and asked her to please call me when she had arrived safely home. She hugged Rella goodbye, shared one last cuddle with our little poodle Bella, and headed out to her car, with me walking step for step with her. She wrapped her arms around me, told me she loved me, and after starting her car, sped off down the driveway. Forty minutes later the telephone rang; it was Angeli calling to say she had gotten home just fine.

A sure fire success in the making, Angeli was an incredible student, filling her schedule with Honors and Advanced Placement classes, while achieving a seriously high GPA. Though an excellent reader, her real strength lay in math and the physical sciences. She handled the most advanced level classes in those areas with ease, cheerfully welcoming the challenges presented therein. Her goal was to become a doctor, she had told me as a sophomore, and she wanted to attend the University of Florida as the first step towards that goal. As she completed her junior year, the end of which I was to retire, she was already looking forward to "nailing" her senior year in order to give herself the best possible chance of getting into UF. Recently, my wife had bought a "Tweety-Bird" themed top, and she thought it would be perfect for Angeli, who confirmed during a telephone call that yes, she'd love to have it. So, after asking her to make sure that her mother would be comfortable with my coming to their home, which she was, I drove down to bring the top to Angeli. Her mother, who works not far from home, had to come to the house to pick up a delivered item that she needed for work, and I had the wonderful opportunity to meet her for the first time in the two years I had known Angeli. Shortly after my arrival, her mom opened the front door, walked into the dining room, and introduced herself. As I took her hand and kissed her on the cheek, she thanked me for always taking such good care of her daughter. I was so genuinely touched by her words. A mother, thanking a person who only two years before had been a stranger, for loving and caring for her child. I responded by saying that to me, Angeli was family, and that it was my pleasure and a true blessing to care for such a wonderful girl. After a quick lunch, and having waited long enough for a partial easing of the powerful rainstorm that had just dumped both rain and hail upon the area, I said goodbye to Angeli and made a break for my car, knowing that my long ride home would likely be a harrowing one, but one that I had to make nonetheless. How right I was!

Throughout this first summer of my retirement, Angeli and I have spoken at least once a week by telephone, and have sent emails and Facebook messages regularly. In the middle of one of our phone conversations, she said "Since you're a retired guy now, and have time to sit around and write books, maybe you can come to one of my soccer or water polo matches to cheer for me." I asked her to email me the schedules for each team, and said that I would try my best to do that. "Don't be surprised if while you're running down the field at a home soccer match at HML you hear a familiar voice screaming "Go Angeli !". She doesn't ask for much, and she deserves that kind of support, so I'll be there. Maybe only for a match or two, but I'll be there.

Dear Mr. Ringler,

You will be missed tremendously by many whose hearts you have touched. In my years as a student I have not once met a teacher, role model like you. Hopefully, I have the privilege to keep in contact with you through the rest of my life, but regardless, I am lucky to have met a man like you in my life. You were always like a father figure to me, and I will never forget and always remember all of the conversations we had and all of the lessons you taught me. I value how we always shared common interests and how as a child you shared the same perspective and lifestyle as I do. There are not very many people left in this world like you and I.

I will forever value your friendship, and I will forever love you.

Angeli

A football player, from the first day of school, he gave me the impression that he was going to be a bit behind the eight ball. He just didn't act or sound like a typical Honors English II student. Not being one to let first impressions dictate to me the true character of a student, I watched and waited as the days and weeks passed, finding that Kevin was in reality a very bright and perceptive boy. I was thrilled to discover the real Kevin. Sure, he sometimes came to class unprepared, as did some other students, and yes, he occasionally drifted off to sleep with his face planted squarely upon the pages of our textbook, but these were shortcomings that I was willing to attribute to his football related activities, and for which I held him fully accountable. It was during class, while studying a piece of literature or discussing an unrelated topic, that Kevin shone through. He more immediately saw things that many of my other students failed to see at first, and demonstrated an incredible depth of understanding of literary concepts that others sometimes failed to grasp. He performed admirably on FCAT Writing, scoring a 5, and rushed to my classroom to share that news, a heartfelt "Yeah, yeah!" exploding from his lips as he proclaimed "I told you I would nail that test, Mr. Ringler."

As a junior at the beginning of the next year, Kevin was informed that he had been awarded some additional credits for a few advanced level courses he had taken while in middle school, and as a result, was now being reclassified as a senior. He would be graduating at the same time I was retiring, and could begin college the following fall. An incredible turn of events! He was positively beaming as he told me the good news, and actually seemed to mature in front of my eyes at that precise moment. Suddenly, he was young man, not a goofy tenth grader, and it showed. During the closing months of his, and my, final year at HML, he stopped by a few extra times to talk with me, telling me he was ready to go and ready to make something of himself. He wished me the very best of everything after I retired, and I wished the same for him after graduation. He's a good one, that Kevin. He'll probably surprise the heck out of everyone by the time he's finished. He certainly surprised the heck out of me.

One of Kevin's classmates in our eighth period English II Honors class was Shanice. A warm and incredibly intelligent girl, Shanice was a wonderful addition to the class. She was a model student, rarely arriving unprepared, and always ready to participate in class discussions. One of her most endearing qualities, at least to me, was her love and appreciation of two of my favorite television shows: "Seinfeld" and "Curb Your Enthusiasm". How unusual it was to find a fifteen year old with a Jerry Seinfeld/Larry David sense of humor. Many Monday afternoons, on her way into class, she would ask if I had seen the previous night's episode of "Curb...", or on other days of the week, any of the syndicated episodes of "Seinfeld". Seinfeld was easy to discuss, but as "Curb..." frequently contained mature themes and language, Shanice and I both instinctively understood what parts we could talk about and what parts we needed to omit. I enjoyed those times with Shanice, and I feel a real sense of loss knowing that we won't be sharing our thoughts about these shows any more. I am thankful, though, to have had her as my student, and I hope to see her when I return to HML for a visit or to perform at Coffee House.

Dear Ringler,

I love you sooooo much. You're my biggest inspiration to do well in school. You got me through my toughest year and I know I could depend on you for anything. You were like a father away from home, except you made it like being at home always. I will never forget you and I'm just grateful to have had been blessed with such a teacher/mentor like you. I am also happy I had FINALLY found someone with an interest in "Seinfeld" and "Curb..." to talk about. I had a great 2 years knowing you Ringler, and it's going to be damn near impossible to find anyone like you to teach English as we know it, with such dedication and compassion. You really opened learning and life into the classroom Ringler.

I LOVE YOU !

Shanice

Chapter 27

A large high school requires many factors to be in place in order to provide a safe environment for its students. Clearly stated and consistently applied rules for students conduct, supported and enforced by administration, faculty, and support staff, help serve to create an atmosphere conducive to effective learning, one in which the "knuckleheads" have been removed from the equation, thus enabling teachers to teach and students to learn. The front line in that battle are the security monitors, men and women who are the eyes and ears of the hallways, and the many secluded alleys tucked away within the perimeter of a school's campus. These good folks patrol their assigned areas, establishing a rapport with the same kids who pass by day after day, and are generally looked upon by the kids as being pretty cool. I've seen them go out of their way to be cooperative and friendly, and I've seen them remain incredibly professional while being taunted or insulted by the few students who will resort to such ignorant behavior. We've had many good ones at HML, but I must share the tales of two of the best I've ever known.

The chief, the peacemaker, the man-mountain. This was Jerry Denson. Jerry served as a security monitor at HML for I don't know how many years, probably fifteen or twenty. A top-level black belt in a number of martial arts areas, but rarely having to call upon his vast skills, Jerry soft-spokenly patrolled the halls, urging kids to move along and get to class. He also served on his own time as an instructor and personal trainer for a few top professional athletes. Jerry and I spent a good deal of time talking, as I would frequently walk a bit with him on my way to or from some main office destination. He was almost my age, outweighed me by at least fifty pounds, and made me feel like his little brother. Even while intervening in the occasional skirmishes that popped up from time to time, Jerry did so with incredible control and dignity, never raising his voice and rarely needing to become at all physical to quell the rising emotions of the two combatants. In recent years, Jerry 's health issues had reduced his ability to serve in his security monitor role, and he eventually left the school to regroup and devote himself to improving his overall health. I'd seen him most recently during one of his visits to school. He made a special visit to my classroom, where we had a good half hour or so to talk and bring each other up to date on our respective lives. He looked good, and he sounded strong, and I knew he was back on the road to being Jerry. When it was time for him to go, he grabbed me in one of his massive grizzly bear hugs and said it had been great to see me before I retired. I told him the exact same thing, and then he walked out of my classroom, leaving me aware that this might possibly be the last time I would see him. Hey, that's the part I hate the most, but accept as necessary. Jerry's contributions to HML may not receive much press, but he was as valuable as anyone in making it a better place.

Jerry had a brother, Kenny Spann, who also served as a security monitor for the school, probably for as long as Jerry had. All of the wonderful attributes that Jerry possessed, Kenny possessed as well. The kids loved him. He played around with them, and joked with them, and in return, they respected him, some even seeking him out for advice. Martial arts prowess and a soft-spoken, peace-loving attitude, just like Jerry, guided Kenny through his daily routine of monitoring the halls and escorting students to waiting administrators. He was a music lover, and he and I spent time discussing my albums, a few of which I had given him copies of to take home. When I first told him that I was going to retire, he asked how he would be able to keep up with my future albums. "Don't worry", I replied, "I'll stay in touch." Believe me, I will definitely stay in touch with Kenny and Jerry, in some way and to some degree, but I'll stay in touch.

Chapter 28

The final week of summer 2011 brought a telephone call that I somehow knew was coming. Doriane Gordon, an amazing English teacher who had been at HML for nine years, and who had become essentially our writing guru, called me to say that an English position had opened up at Palmetto Senior High, and she had accepted it. As in my case, Dori and her husband and daughter lived quite a distance from HML, though to the south rather than to the north, of school. Her mornings had become increasingly complicated as her daughter approached kindergarten age, and she was looking to uncomplicate things a bit by transferring to a school much closer to home. Palmetto was the perfect choice, as her husband was already employed there. When the opportunity presented itself, she had to take it.

Dori was the teacher to whom we had assigned the bulk of our writing classes, and she was the "go to" person regarding all things writing. Of course, she shared with me anything I needed to be aware of as department chair, but I trusted her implicitly and deferred to her whenever I could. Over the years, Dori and I had developed a daughter/father relationship. Most recently, her classroom was next to mine, and we often shared time chatting during common plan periods, covering a range of topics from school to family to everything in between. There were times when Dori would storm into my room, seething about something or other, and times when she would just stop by to give me a hug or ask if I wanted coffee, which she always had brewing in her room. Sometimes we just sat and shared our dreams and our heartbreaks with each other, astounding triumphs in class or the loss of family members. Some folks at HML may have found Dori to be a bit aloof, but I found her, and still find her, warm and caring and fiercely loyal. My God, every year, the night before our tenth grade students were to take the FCAT Writing Assessment, she would stay up until who knows when, making fresh pancakes to bring to school the next morning, I mean hundreds of them, along with syrup and a variety of juices, just to make sure her students had a good breakfast before the test. Her students loved her so much, and they worked as hard as they had ever worked, just to please her. When she left HML, many of them were deeply saddened by her departure, and asked me to say "hi" to her for them the next time I spoke with her. She had held them to the most stringent writing standards, and the results achieved by her students had always proven what a wonderful teacher she was.

I drove down to school a few days before teachers had to report as Dori had called to tell me she would be coming to her classroom to pack up a number of things she would be taking with her to Palmetto, wondering if I'd like to come and see if there was anything I would like to keep for the next year's writing classes. For the short time I was with her in her room, I was able to glean a few items that would undoubtedly be helpful. More importantly, we had a chance to talk about her move and how much easier things would now be for her. Once she had boxed up the majority of her belongings, I helped her transfer them to her car, loaded them in her trunk and back seat, and then we hugged for a few moments as we said goodbye to each other. Dori, like many of my students, was family, and her leaving was a tough one to handle. Fortunately, we stayed in touch quite frequently during her first year at Palmetto via telephone and emails, and when I first told her of my decision to retire, she said that the first thing she and her family wanted to do was to come up to my home and take my wife and me out for a celebratory dinner. We did indeed get together a few weeks after I retired, and had the most wonderful time. My wife Rella had very briefly met Dori years ago at a school picnic, possibly Dori's first year at HML, but she had spoken with her a few times on the telephone. Dori, ever the drama kid, kept her completely entertained the entire time they were with us, as did Dori's daughter and husband, and by the time they left for home, It was clear that Rella was going to miss them too. Dori and I have since spoken a number of times throughout the summer of 2012, and will continue to do so as the school year unfolds. The good folks at Palmetto have a real gem on their hands, and I'm sure they know that only too well.

Chapter 29

Jose's second year at HML, 2011-2012, was my third year back as Language Arts Department Chair, the position I had initially held from 1987-1991. As the Reading and Writing portions of FCAT were such significant accountability measurements, Language Arts was an area under intense scrutiny from all directions. As the Reading Department primarily handled the students whose reading skills were most deficient, that department was likewise regularly in the "lens" of the school and district. With the tenth grade FCAT Reading and Writing results being the primary areas of focus, followed by the Reading results of the ninth grade, and eleventh and twelfth grade "re-takers", students who had previously taken and failed the Reading portion of the FCAT, Language Arts had more than its share of responsibility. Every grade level English "curriculum pacing guide" created by the district was dominated by FCAT infused skill building materials and activities. Faced with the daunting task of balancing the teaching of literature and writing with the demands of the FCAT, the good folks at the District Language Arts area tried their level best to accommodate both areas, but FCAT always took precedence. I was so proud of my department for their commitment to the literature, and I found myself in a constant balancing act, trying to have my administration see the powerful benefits of having my English teachers do what they do best, while satisfying the demands of the FCAT. I felt so strongly, as did the rest of my department, that the FCAT skills would come along for the ride with the reading of the literature. The problem, as the administration saw it, was that there were so many lower level readers scattered throughout our English classes that there was no way that those students could absorb the FCAT skills necessary if they could not even comfortably read the literature. I understood and respected their logic, but still remained convinced that if the students were exposed to great, perhaps sometimes only good, literature, in an academic environment fostered by good teachers and stronger students, then even those weaker students might have their "fires lit", and become more willing to read, which in turn would better prepare them for FCAT. It's a tough call, it always was. It was clear to me that teaching FCAT skills in isolation wasn't the answer, so approaching it from the perspective of a literature-based foundation just seemed to be the more likely path towards success. No kid is excited about practicing FCAT skills, but many kids, even less than successful ones, have been turned on by literature. Ultimately, we all taught the literature, or as much of it as we could get to in light of the FCAT preparatory barrage that hung over us like a sword in our classrooms. We also covered the FCAT skills as required, primarily using the literature as the foundation upon which the skills were introduced and revisited, and I believed that was the best we could do given the circumstances.

The "other" component of FCAT that was long ago more of an "add-on" than a serious player, was the FCAT Writing Assessment. Originally designed to test a student's ability to write at a minimal level, the test had been revised and revamped over the years, with the state believing that a passing score on the test was indicative of writing mastery. The state's own FCAT Writing guides were filled with required writing components that would only lead to stilted, mechanical, and unimaginative pieces of writing, but the state always needs an instrument by which to hold school accountable, no matter how faulty those instruments might be, and so the FCAT Writing

Assessment served, and continues to serve, as that tool. Recently, the winds of change began blowing across the mountains, rivers, prairies, and sand dunes of the country, and the concept of creating national education standards took hold. Whatever standards Johnny was held to in Missouri would be the same standards to which Ashley would be held in Florida. The idea has its merits, and many countries with far more successful educational systems in place than the United States, have been utilizing their own national standards for decades. In keeping with this growing movement, knowing that national standards would supposedly be in place by 2014-2015, the state of Florida decided to seriously upgrade the FCAT Writing Assessment. Discussed earlier in the book, the statewide results of the first year of testing on the newly revised FCAT Writing were disastrous for many reasons, most of them the fault of the state. In any case, Jose Bueno knew that HML had to do something to provide its students with the best chance for success on not only the 2011-2012 administration of the test, but on future administrations of the FCAT Writing Assessment as well. And so, in December 2011, shortly before we were to leave for our Winter Break, Jose stopped by my classroom and asked me to see him when I had a moment. I had no idea what he was planning, but I soon found out. As the new emphasis on writing was now going full speed ahead, and as I was that year teaching a number of Creative Writing (translated as FCAT Writing Prep) classes in addition to my English II classes, and had two additional teachers teaching Creative Writing classes as well, his plan was to start a new Writing Department, with me serving as department chair of course. (I would also continue serving as Foreign Language Department Chair, a position I had been told at the close of the previous year was to be mine.) His news took me by surprise, and I immediately had to mull this concept around in my own head for a minute before responding. When I had digested his idea, I said that I saw where he was going, and understood the move. I also said that this was going to take me away from a position I loved, and a group of people with whom I loved working, but that I was willing to make the change and lead the new department. Jose's next question to me, "Who do we get to replace you as Language Arts Department Chair?", led to a brief brainstorming session between the two of us, after which we decided that we would simply put it "out there" to the department and see who stepped forward.

After revealing our new plan to all of my Language Arts and Foreign Language teachers, and once the buzzing had faded for the moment, I said that the task now was to have one of them assume my responsibilities by the new year or shortly thereafter. Overall, two of them expressed a possible interest, but circumstances would prevent one of them from pursuing the matter any further. The other candidate, Michelle Ruiz, was sitting next to me that day at lunch, when she leaned over to whisper to me. "I think I'd like to try for the position" she said.

Michelle Ruiz was a graduate of Hialeah-Miami Lakes Senior High School, had been one the school's top performing students, and sometime after graduating from college had returned to HML, but this time as an English teacher. Diminutive in stature, but spirited and willing to accept a variety of responsibilities, Michelle had served as our yearbook advisor for nine years, while primarily teaching eleventh grade classes. She had spoken with me a couple of times since my return as department chair as to the possibility of stepping away from yearbook, as the duties and constant deadlines of that position had simply worn her out. We had become close over the years, with her sharing with me many of the difficult situations she found herself facing, and I wanted so badly for her to be happy. She had a new husband, a son from her previous marriage, a less than amiable relationship with her ex-husband when it came to the visitation of their son, and truly needed to have less weight upon her tiny shoulders. Fortunately, we had recently brought on board a wonderful new teacher named Janine Castillo, who had served as Yearbook Advisor for the half year she had been at her previous school, Barbara Goleman Senior High. Prior to the 2010-2011 school year, I was able to have Michelle moved to a newly opened ninth grade spot, and have Janine installed as the new Yearbook Advisor. A perfect switch, especially as Michelle had shared with us at the end of the previous year the wonderful news that she was expecting her second child, a daughter, who would make her debut during August of 2010. Once little Lucia had made her appearance, and after a maternity leave that ended in time for the beginning of the second marking period, Michelle was back at HML, working as hard as ever with her new ninth grade classes. Despite the FCAT pressures now thrust upon her, she was always incredibly diligent, and focused upon finding the right balance between teaching literature and incorporating the required FCAT skills included in the district curriculum. She completed the remainder of that year, and had completed half of the next, when I announced my move to the newly created Writing Department.

At lunch that day, when she first whispered to me that she was interested in replacing me, I think I was prouder of her than I had ever been before. I returned the whisper, asking why she thought she might like to "have a go" at the position. "I sometimes feel so overwhelmed by things around here, and I think that as department chair I would feel like I'd have a deeper understanding of what's going on, and at least have some control over things." I agreed with her logic, and said that we would have to discuss this a bit more. Once I had presented her with a number of leadership scenarios, and had found her responses to be exactly those I would expect from a leader-in-waiting, I told her that I would speak to Jose, letting him know that we had found my replacement. Here was a girl who, despite her fears and concerns about accountability and confrontation, was willing to put herself smack dab in the middle of potentially a firestorm of both. I did indeed speak with Jose that afternoon, expressed my confidence in Michelle, and recommended her as my replacement. A couple of afternoons after, as I was walking towards the teacher's parking lot, Michelle, or "Little One" as I had been calling her for a number of years, walked up to me and said that she had been given the position. She was excited as could be about it, though I could see the apprehension in her face. When I asked her what Jose had said during the interview, she replied that there had been no interview, that Jose had just asked her to stop by his office after school, at which point he said that I had strongly recommended her for the position. As a result, she was to be my replacement and I would serve as her mentor. Michelle and I would speak of department chair "stuff" on an ongoing basis, there was always something I needed to say to her or she needed to ask of me. She was a quick learner, and so bright and perceptive that I had every confidence that she would grow into the position in time. I continued to keep a watchful eye on the department, and continued to "mentor" Michelle until the day I left HML for the last time, with a promise to her that I would always be there for her even after I had gone, knowing that "Little One" will probably just figure it all out for herself anyway.

Chapter 30

One afternoon, a month or so into my final year at HML, my dear friend and colleague Karen Stemer entered my classroom to talk with me, but finding me in the middle of interviewing a prospective Writing teacher, she said she would see me another time and left the room. As it turned out, Karen had stopped by to inform me that she had been diagnosed with breast cancer, and needed to talk about it. (Understand that upon my arrival at HML so many years ago, and for the next few years thereafter, Karen and I were not exactly the best of friends, though I am unsure whether or not she would remember that. Over the course of many years that followed, that had changed, and we had certainly become closer, if not exactly best buddies. The last decade or so found us closer still, with more open conversations and more revealed thoughts and feelings passing between us. Plus, we were both Jewish, and as members of a very small grouping of Jewish faculty and staff at the school, there was that special bond as well.) "Breast cancer? How the hell did that happen?" Here was a woman who stayed on top of her health like a crazy person, with an ongoing parade of doctor's appointments from one week to the next. Okay, maybe that's a bit of an exaggeration, but not by much! Once she had described the entire range of events leading up to her diagnosis, all I could do was to hug her and tell her that she was going to be okay. She sadly claimed that she wasn't sure if she wanted to fight this battle, to which I said "Bull...t! You're going to fight like hell, and you're going to beat this. No question in my mind." As Karen knew that I had recently written a song for HML's beloved Ann Zirkle, I figured that this was a time to lighten things up a bit, so I exclaimed "Besides, I'm not writing a song about you!"

This brought a smile and a few tears of happiness to her face, and I was so glad that my foray into levity had helped, even if for only a moment. Endless visits to an endless line of doctors eventually provided Karen with "the plan of attack", and after arranging a medical leave from HML, she bravely faced every facet of her treatment, up to and including the multi-week barrage of radiation treatments she had to undergo during the summer of 2012. Having vowed to return to HML for her scheduled final year of teaching, she remained true to her word, with the beginning of the 2012-2013 school year starting as so many years before had started, with Karen Stemer standing at the door of her classroom, welcoming her seniors to their soon to unfold journey into the world of British Literature.

Chapter 31

Once I had announced that I would be retiring in June 2012, many of my current sophomores, my final group of students, seemed to become even a bit more attached to me than usual. These were the kids who were with me in English II Honors or Regular, Creative Writing, and in some cases, both classes. At times, my Regular English class and a few of my Writing classes made me think back to my first years at HML; some students cared a great deal about their work, and some not at all. My Creative Writing classes contained a mixture of higher and lower achieving tenth graders, and at times the differences were frighteningly all too clear. After all these years, there were still disaffected kids who just wouldn't make an effort to improve their chances for a decent future, choosing instead to meander through their lives, thinking that somehow it would magically all work out for them. Despite my frequent private, patient and supportive conversations with them, and my many parent telephone calls to their homes, these few kids willingly decided that failure was an option. I told them how much I hated that they had chosen this path for themselves, and how I knew how successful they could be if they'd only try, but I just couldn't get them to see the light. Overall however, most of my students were dedicated and hard-working, and at the very least understood what I had been trying all year to have them understand; that it was up to them to succeed, and that, as clichéd as it may have sounded, what they put into school was exactly what they would get out of it.

As I've mentioned in another chapter, as close as some students and I have become during the year that they are with me, it has frequently been the next year when our relationships have grown even stronger, despite their not actually being with me in a class. They pass by to talk and share a hug, run to show me their report cards, keep me up-to-date on things in general, ask me to teach them how to tie their ties, even sign up to serve as one of my teacher aides. I knew I wouldn't have that opportunity with my final group of kids, and that the best I could hope for would be to give them as much of myself as I could in my last year, and hope some of it would "stick". Of course, I also realized that there were a number of them who would stay in touch after I had gone, and that provided me some degree of comfort. I definitely found myself holding the kids who hugged me a little longer, and shaking their hands a little harder, when they left my classroom. This whole retirement "thing", leaving my kids behind, was definitely getting the better of me as I approached the last few months of the year.

Every year brought to me a host of shining stars, and that final year was no exception. There were Honors kids who were already on the path to success, taking advanced level classes and participating in a wide range of extra-curricular activities, and there were Regular level kids who had not only set their sights on becoming more successful students, but were willing to pay the price to achieve that goal. Though I would love to discuss each and every one of them, my focus will have to be upon just a handful.

Nicholas and I found very early on in the year that we both shared a passion for music. He was more than excited to discover that not only had I recorded a number of albums of my own original songs, plus a Beatles tribute album that previous summer, all of which were on I-Tunes and Amazon.com, but that since 2006 nearly two dozen of my recordings had received limited airplay on smaller radio stations in a number of countries, including the United States. Nicholas was a guitarist in the making, a very talented one, and we spent a great deal of time discussing guitars and the entire recording process I followed in creating my albums. A strong student taking both my English II Honors and Creative Writing classes, he was clearly on his way up at HML. His insights and discussions in class showed exactly how bright and perceptive he was, and he became one of the students upon whom I most depended. On most days, as I stood in the hallway outside of my classroom between classes, I would see Nicholas walking calmly towards me, guitar in hand, greeting me with an understated "Hey Mr. Ringler." Within seconds, I could hear him playing The Beatles "Blackbird", or some other piece he had so beautifully made part of his repertoire. A quick glance into my room revealed him sitting quietly at his desk, delicately picking the notes on his guitar, playing each section over and over until he felt satisfied enough to place the guitar at the side of my room and return to his seat, waiting for me to enter and for class to begin. At one of the Coffee House fundraiser events, one at which Nicholas and his band mate were rehearsing the tunes they were going to perform , I had just finished setting up my equipment and was running through some of my songs, when Nicholas yelled across to me "Hey Mr. Ringler, let's jam!" I began to play a bluesy chord structure, to which Nicholas responded with some lead guitar, and then we reversed roles and I played lead while he strummed away. We had a grand old time for a good ten minutes, then abruptly brought things to a close as the door was opened, letting in the students and adults who had been waiting outside for the show to begin.

As the school year came to a close, Nicholas insisted that he was going to stay in touch after I had gone, and stay in touch he has.

We have communicated by email about new albums and his own new music, as well as a few school related matters. If I do indeed perform at the next Coffee House, Nicholas will undoubtedly be the first in line to greet me. He's a great kid, and I miss our time together in my two classes.

Randy was another of my superstar students that year. He was bright, mature, and intellectually curious about a variety of topics. On more than one occasion, he would raise his hand to discuss something he had read, or had seen on television that in some way related to our class topic. He genuinely wanted to share this information, though he occasionally appeared to be almost apologetic to the class for having done so. Many things interested him, he knew a bit about a number of them, and I was as interested in them as he was, so the combination worked. Science, history, sports; we covered them all. He also had very good taste in music, at least by my standards, and we often discussed the music of an assortment of classic rock bands, with him knowing much more about that than most kids of his generation. His dad, it seems, was the catalyst for this, having been a fan of such music for decades. I had never met his dad, but I knew I liked him already.

"Don't worry Ringler, I've got the FCAT Writing covered." These were Randy's words to me the last time he was with me in class prior to the day that all sophomores were scheduled to take the newest version of this state assessment. Months later, when the outrageously flawed results were released by the state, I received the list of scores for every test-taker in the school. FCAT Writing was scored on a scale of 1-6, with 6 being the highest, and consequently a score attained by only a select few of our students over the years, though that number had increased over the past few years. As I tracked the names of my students on the list, I stopped at Randy's score. He had received a 6, one of only a handful of my kids to do so that year. I was incredibly proud of him for that. When Randy appeared at my classroom door, he was grinning from ear to ear as he had already been informed of his exemplary score by his Creative Writing teacher. "I told you I was going to nail that test." "Yes, Randy, you most certainly did."

One of the first telephone calls I received after retiring was from Randy. He was calling to see how I was doing, and to discuss a concert he had recently attended. After we had covered everything, I told him that he should feel free to call or email whenever he wished. We've been in touch a few more times since then, and he has every intention of seeing me at Coffee House. That will be a treat, for both of us.

There are two people whom I address as "Little One": Michelle Ruiz, who bravely took over for me as Language Arts Department Chair when I moved over to the Writing Department Chair slot, and a delightful student named Natalie who was with me in my last year for both English II Honors and Creative Writing. No bigger than a minute, Natalie was one of the brightest, most perceptive students I've ever known. An extremely sensitive and curious girl, Natalie came to depend upon me for answers; answers to questions about class topics, and answers to questions about life. When something piqued her interest or confused her, up went her hand. On the occasions when the class was working independently, she would quietly walk over to my desk to share a thought or ask a question about some insightful observation she had made. I loved those moments, the moments when she would reveal the profound, searching Natalie, the girl possessed of so much depth and heart. As the year progressed, the more areas we discussed, and the more in tune we became.

Very early on, I discovered how easily distracted she could be, and conversely, how quickly she could disappear into a book that she might be reading while the class was working at some other task. She saw that in herself, cognizant of how easily she could withdraw into "Natalie's World", as I labeled it. I never admonished her for zoning out, I could see how that was simply a part of her, though a part that I attempted to have her become more aware of so as not to fall behind. She always said she knew that she would have to work on that aspect of her life, and there was some improvement by the year's end. How wonderful it was to see an exceptionally aware fifteen year old kid consciously work towards self-correction. I was so proud of her for that, and for so many other things as well, and I almost never let a day go by without telling her.

A powerfully expressive and intuitive reader, and a deeply thoughtful and highly detailed writer, Natalie was a joy to teach. Beloved by her fellow students, she was a most sociable girl, but there was a more introverted and private side to her as well, and we talked a great deal about that early in the summer. Happily, Natalie was excited about beginning a volunteer position as a counselor at a local camp program, and in no time at all would find herself with a new group of "summer" friends with whom she would spend the next couple of months. We have been in touch on a number of occasions since I left HML, and I will continue to follow her progress, and talk with her, about everything she wants to share with me. She is my little Natalie, a part of my family, and we will stay in touch.

Mr. Ringler,

I wanted to begin by saying thank you, thank you for helping me become a better person, for helping me to see the good in myself, for always believing in me in my times of self-doubt, for always putting a smile on my face, even on my worst days. I can honestly say no teacher in my 10 years of grade school has ever had such a positive influence on me until I entered the tenth grade. My sophomore year will always be one to remember after having such an outstanding, caring, and extremely wise English teacher. Ringler, you are one of a kind. I can bet that many teachers here at HML envy that bond you share amongst all your students, and even those kids who graduated but still come in contact with you. You have this unique ability to bring warmth into any atmosphere, whether it be a classroom or you just simply standing in the hallway, waving at your students as they stroll throughout the hall. You have so much positivity within you that it almost seems to bring out the best in us. In all honesty, it breaks my heart knowing that you're retiring this year, being that this is the year I met you.

I hope you have the best retirement, or a wonderful one at least. I can assure you that great things will continue to come your way as years go by. You deserve the best. One last thank you for opening my eyes to the things I was too blind to see. I could never thank you enough.

P.S. I will be sure to contact you this summer, "Mr. Yearbook". Ha ha!

Love always,

Natalie

"Hi Grandpa". Not the usual greeting from a student to a teacher, but in the case of Chavely, it was the loving and affectionate label that she assigned to me. Yes, I am a grandpa, and yes, my grandchildren address me as such. In Chavely's eyes, however, the title was not borne of age, but of wisdom and respect. At least, that was how she explained it to me the first time she said it. Either that, or she was just calling me an old man! Knowing Chavely as I did, I went with her explanation. Every time she called me Grandpa, she was telling me that she loved me, and how can that be an insult?

Chavely was in one of my Creative Writing classes. She was a cheerful and positive thinking girl, filled with hopeful thoughts and beautiful dreams which I could hear in her voice and see in her eyes. Like most girls her age, she was a true romantic, and she reveled in hearing stories of how I had met my wife, how long we had been married, and what our children were up to these days. Her writing was filled with warmth and depth, and demonstrated a level of maturity that was rare among many of her peers. During independent writing activities, I would often find her painstakingly searching for just the right words to write, she cared that much about the thoughts she was putting down on paper. As I always invited my kids to bring their papers to me when they had questions, or simply wanted a quick critique, I frequently found Chavely standing by my side as I sat in a student desk, my usual spot during such activities, her arm resting comfortably upon my shoulder as she waited for me to read her work and respond. She locked on to every word I said, her eyes dual laser beams of focused concentration. Every suggestion, every idea, every word I said, she took them and made them her own, incorporating each into her writing, seeing their sense and their purpose.

Chavely emailed me a few times not long after school ended, excited about her upcoming volunteer job working with younger students at a nearby school. Side by side with her best friend Sarah, another wonderful girl, she was ready to tackle whatever responsibilities came with the position, and was anxious for the show to begin. Later in the summer, a follow up email from her filled me in on her progress at the job, and as expected, she was enjoying herself and gaining valuable experience. Chavely will be among those kids I miss the most. Her warmth, her wit, her cheerful smile, I'll miss them all. It will likely be the distant, fading sound of her "Love you Grandpa" that I will miss the most.

Ringler, oh dear Ringler,

It makes me sad that I was only able to spend one year with you, and just one year of knowing you. To put negatives aside, I'm way more than thankful to at least have had the opportunity to have met you. I'll always remember you by your loving, generous charisma. When I say you're like a grandpa, I hope you know it's not by wrinkles or years on your back, but by your wise words, stories, and caring self. If there's a teacher to thank and love, definitely, it would be you. I can sit here and write out all of the amazing things and details, but there truly aren't enough words to describe such a marvelous man. Thursday, if I'm not able to see you, I just want to wish you the best in your now "stress free of work" life. Enjoy the years to come, because someone like you deserves that and much, much more. We will all miss you, but we all understand your reasons and it's for the best, and here it is.

I love you Grandpa!

Chavely

It's the quiet ones, the ones who make you feel like you're pulling teeth, that sometimes turn out to be the superstars. Annaly was a quiet one. Another student in my eighth period Creative Writing class, on the first day of school she unassumingly floated into my room, sat down, and for the most part, remained voiceless for the entire period. I wasn't even sure if she could speak at all. With each passing day, however, I began to hear her voice, just a bit here and a bit there, but a voice nonetheless. Her writing showed incredible promise, though I suspected that she wasn't exactly putting her best foot forward with each assignment.

Words of encouragement, and an insistence upon their giving me their best work, usually resulted in many of my students caring that much more about their writing, about how they were representing themselves, and Annaly began to live up to the promise I had seen in her from the start. She was a strong writer, if not always a highly motivated one, and her ideas and relative command of the tools of writing impressed me. If she would only take the time to give me her best, her work would be amazing, I told her on more than one occasion. As was the case with so many kids, the longer they knew me, and the better they understood me, the more willing they were to show me what they could really do, and Annaly was no exception, though her starting point was higher than most. The year rolled on, she became a bit more open and comfortable talking with me, and her work became stronger, if not yet her absolute best. She questioned me about my life and I found out more about hers. She watched me perform at Coffee House, and I believe that seeing me play guitar and singing changed her perception of me even further. I was Mr. Ringler, her teacher, but I was also Mike Ringler, a rock and roll guy, and she connected with that. She seemed genuinely touched by my plan to retire, and demanded a guarantee that I would come to her graduation in two years. "Don't worry, I'll be there."

In the short term, hopefully I'll see Annaly again at Coffee House, and we'll spend a few minutes talking, and catching up on things. I hope to find out that she's at the top of her game; that she's firmly on the path to becoming one of HML's finest students. Somehow, I think that's exactly what I'll find.

My sophomore year wouldn't have been the same without you Mr. Ringler. All of your stories, compliments about my writing, and lessons, were amazing! It's a shame that you won't be present for the rest of my high school years, but I will be delighted to see you at Coffee House and my graduation. Thank you for making me more passionate about my writing. It's been an honor to be in your eighth period class. Oh! And thank you for teaching me about nutrition and not to eat red meat; because of you I'll live longer! So, have an amazing, wonderful retirement and I'll hopefully see you next year. You'll always be in my thoughts and prayers.

P.S. you were my favorite teacher this year, in case you didn't know. I love you.

God Bless,

Annaly

Chapter 32

There are schools "out there" that know exactly how to play the school grade "game"; how to pick up valuable points to be applied to their total school grade formula, thus leading to a higher school grade. Instead of depending solely upon the FCAT results as a means by which to receive a satisfactory grade from the state, schools recognize that points can be secured through the introduction or expansion of advanced academic programs, ie: "dual enrollment", wherein students take college classes concurrently with their high school classes, and a variety of state certification programs whereby students who successfully pass those programs' respective certification tests garner extra points for a school towards the school's report card grade. There are numerous other special programs that can also lead to these cherished "extra points", and fortunately for HML, Jose Bueno looked closely at expanding our existing "extra point" programs, while seeking to "bring in" new ones as well. I had said publicly for years that if HML was indeed ever to have a chance to regain some of its original luster, it would have to become a "something" school. Jose knew this, and not only did he guide HML closer to becoming a "dual enrollment" school, but he also "landed" a very prestigious advanced level program for the start of the 2012-2013 school year, "I-Prep", making HML one of only five schools in the district to offer this, hopefully, student-attracting program. Much greater emphasis was also placed upon vastly increasing the number of students actively preparing for "industry certification" testing, and those numbers increased sharply. With Jose's ability to clearly see the whole picture, it seemed that his second year at HML would give the school a much better chance of attaining the elusive

"C" grade, or perhaps, one even higher. Unfortunately, while elementary and middle school grades are completed either by the end of each school year, or shortly thereafter, grades for high schools take much longer to calculate, primarily due to the expanded factors recently incorporated into the grade formula, and possibly due to the inability of the state to figure out its own system in the first place, a failing previously noted previously in this book. Consequently, the school grades for 2011-2012 will not be released until possibly January 2013, so the results of Jose's plan of attack will remain unknown until then. Having retired, I am "out of the loop", but I will certainly be notified once HML has received its 2011-2012 grade, as the FCAT results of my own individual classes, plus those of my former departmental colleagues, will either have contributed to, or detracted from, that grade. Having been there to see all of the steps taken to bolster our chances of moving up once again, my money's on a "C", but with Jose Bueno in charge, you just never know. Those extra points he helped to guide us towards may yet take HML into "B" territory!

Chapter 33

Graduation 2012, and there were so many students to whom I
needed to say goodbye. I knew from all of my previous
graduations that it would be almost impossible to find all of
those students once the ceremony had ended, as they usually
dissipated into the atmosphere that surrounds Florida
International University's athletic arena, meeting with friends
and family in far off corners of the great lawns, or gathered in
the confines of hidden hallways. How lost I must have always
looked in the past, circling the outside perimeter of F.I.U. in
search of my new graduates; exactly the way I must have looked
that hot June day as I searched for Victoria and her family.
Many minutes passed, and I was preparing to call it a day, when
I spotted Victoria, standing with her family and her dear friend
Karina, grouped together around the corner from where I had
set my eagle eyes in motion. "Mr. Ringler!!!", came the shout
from the wonderful girl I had known for four years. Navigating
through the throng of soon-to-be freshmen-again students and
adults that lined the walkway, I was soon in the middle of a hug
fest from all directions: first Victoria, then her parents, then
Karina, who had been my student at HML as well a few years
ago before transferring to another school (boo !), and finally,
her grandparents. Victoria was quite obviously overwhelmed by
the surreal nature of graduation. Four years prior, she had been
a bright and sensitive fourteen year old child, a child who
quickly felt comfortable enough to share her problems and
concerns with me. Her sweet, giggly laughter during class still
echoes in my ears even today. Now, she had blossomed into a
confident and beautiful young woman, about to leave childhood
things behind and take the next step towards her future. We

posed together for pictures, with Karina right there with us, and the two girls and I talked for a while about graduation "stuff". Her mom and dad soon joined in the conversation, followed in short order by her grandparents. Her mom had long ago welcomed me into "the family", always stopping by to talk with me at each year's Open House, despite the fact that Victoria had only been my student in ninth grade English I Honors, though she continued working me with me closely for the next three years as a teacher aide. Imagine how honored and touched I felt when during Victoria's senior year, her mother said that she wanted me to continue being a part of Victoria's life after she graduated. Her dad, whom I had only recently met at the National Honor Society Breakfast as his daughter had been a member, thanked me for the time I had spent working with Victoria over the past four years. A bit of conversation with her grandparents, a few final hugs, and it was time to leave them.

A week after graduation, I received an email from Victoria, explaining that she and her parents were out of town, visiting her dad's sister who had recently had a stroke, and that she'd get back to me when they returned. Being an ambitious student, Victoria had registered for two college classes for the summer, and between that and her part-time job, we communicated by email and occasionally by telephone, but were unable to get together until just a few days before she was to start her first full college semester. Late that final Friday morning, my wife and I drove to her house, and found her dad preparing to leave on a business related matter. He enthusiastically shook my hand and hugged me, and after being introduced to my wife, embraced her as well. I love her dad. He's a kind and generous man, and it is so obvious how much he adores his daughter. He was sorry he had to go at that moment, but he invited me to come down with my wife on another day to have coffee with the family. My wife, who had spoken a time or two to Victoria on the telephone in my classroom, finally had the chance to meet her in person. There was a sight to see: my five foot tall wife hugging the five foot eight Victoria. A brief tour of her house followed, and then we were off to lunch. Two hours can disappear in the blink of an eye, much like childhood, and we were soon saying goodbye to Victoria in front of her house, with an invitation for her to visit us at our home in the near future. She was so excited about that prospect, and suggested that perhaps she could bring Karina, and Maria, another of my closest students. "Definitely" I replied, and after we had held each other for a few moments, and had said our "I love you-s.", she hugged my wife. Then I started my car, waved goodbye, and back home we went, Victoria growing smaller and smaller in my rearview mirror.

Dear Mr. Ringler,

Where do I even begin? Coming into HML as a freshman I was confused, naïve, and vulnerable. Thank God I was blessed with you as my English teacher! You instantly became the person I could run to for whatever reason. You put up with my insane laugh attacks, endless talking in class, and my "oh-so-dramatic" boyfriend problems. LOL! (I don't know how you did it!) I have been so blessed to have been able to build a relationship with you throughout my years at HML, and now as a senior graduating, I can say that you are another father figure in my life. I'm not going to get too emotional because I know I will be seeing you often. I love you so much. Thank you for everything you've done for me so far.

Xoxo, Victoria

Chapter 34

When I left HML I left behind children and adults for whom I cared deeply, some whom I truly loved very much. You can't work with so many for so long and not develop attachments to them, well, with the exception of those whom you really could have done without, I suppose. One becomes close to those next to him or her in the trenches, or in an educator's case, the classrooms and offices, that make up a school. At the end of the year faculty breakfast on the last day of school, after listening to the accolades accorded me by my principal and a few of my oldest English Department colleagues and friends, Michael Garcia and Karen Stemer, it was my turn to address the audience. With my career flashing in front of my eyes as I spoke, I recalled for them the time I had gone downtown and demanded to see someone in Personnel right then and there, knowing that the district was indeed looking to fill a growing number of open teaching positions. When Hialeah-Miami Lakes Senior High was mentioned as one of the schools with an opening, I told the audience that I had said "That's the one I want", and an interview was quickly arranged for the next morning. Having now come full circle, staring my own future right in the face, I said proudly that I had made the right choice on that day in February 1984, the absolute right decision, and that I had never regretted a single moment of my time at Hialeah-Miami Lakes Senior High School. I stared into the faces of my colleagues and friends from my Language Arts, Writing, and Foreign Language Departments, and into the faces of so many other teachers and staff I had known, and said my final goodbyes. That was the hardest part for me, saying goodbye.

The summer has ended and the new school year has begun, except this time, I wasn't there on the first day. As I always knew it would, Hialeah-Miami Lakes Senior High School has carried on without me, relegating me to nothing more than a pleasant memory, a photograph on the Teacher of the Year wall in the Media Center, or a loving thought in the hearts and minds of those remaining students and employees with whom I spent the final years of my time at the school. The students who filled my email, and my life, with messages throughout the summer, have returned to the place I loved for so many years, ready to take the next step in their progression towards college and a career after that. For those who graduated when I retired, the fall college semester has also begun, a time in which they will come to realize how fortunate they are to be continuing their education, but also a time for them to remember the years they spent at HML. They will miss them, for a while at least, and then they will boldly move ahead towards their futures, with the memories of their high school years tucked neatly and securely within their hearts. That is where I will keep my HML memories, tucked neatly and securely within my own heart, forever, and for all time.

About My Music

As mentioned in the book, I have recorded eight albums of original songs, with a few cover versions included here and there. Since 2006, I have been fortunate enough to have had many of my songs played on small radio stations in a number of countries, including Australia, Canada, England, Germany, Italy, Japan, and the United States. Two of my songs have been featured on charity CD's in England, and one, which I wrote specifically for the project, was included as the featured song on a bonus CD accompanying a book written about John Lennon.

My sixth album, *VI*, was beautifully reviewed in the April 2011 issue of *The Big Takeover* magazine, and my newest album as of the date of this book's publication, *There Comes A Moment,* will be reviewed in that same magazine's November 2012 issue.

The title track from the newest album was written as my goodbye to the career, and the children, I loved so deeply. Below are the lyrics to that song:

There Comes A Moment

Though it hurts me so to say it, it's time to step away

From a lifetime filled with love, and smiling faces

I suppose there comes a moment, when the curtains must be drawn

As the window closes softly right behind them

They will all stay deep inside me, forever in my heart

Even those I should forget won't be forgotten

I'm a better man for knowing them

I knew that from the start

They may have taught me more than I taught them

They made me look inside myself.

There's a new door I must walk through

Though I'm not sure where it leads

It's just waiting for me now to find the right key

I suppose there'll come a moment

When that door will open wide

And the new road I'm to follow will lay before me

And I'll walk that road with confidence

No fear of the unknown

That's just one of the rare gifts of growing older

When I find that place that feels like me

The sun will light the sky

And I'll hear the whispers on the wind

That I heard oh, so long ago

Though it hurts me so to say it

It's time to step away

From a lifetime filled with love, and smiling faces

I suppose there comes a moment, when the curtains must be drawn

As the window closes softly right behind them

Lyrics and music: Mike Ringler

©2012

Printed in Great Britain
by Amazon

69814232R00108